Wishbone Wisdom

EMORY BELLARD— TEXAS FOOTBALL VISIONARY

Coach Emory Bellard
Father of the Wishbone Offense

As Told to Al Pickett

To Kevin

Emory Bellard

Wishbone Wisdom

EMORY BELLARD—
TEXAS FOOTBALL VISIONARY

Coach Emory Bellard
Father of the Wishbone Offense

As Told to Al Pickett

State House Press

Buffalo Gap, Texas

Library of Congress Cataloging-in-Publication Data

Bellard, Emory.
  Wishbone wisdom : Emory Bellard, Texas football visionary /
by Emory Bellard as told to Al Pickett.
    p. cm.
  Includes bibliographical references and index.
  ISBN-13: 978-1-933337-41-8 (pbk. : alk. paper)
  ISBN-10: 1-933337-41-9 (pbk. : alk. paper)
  1. Football–Offense. 2. Football–Coaching. 3. Football–Texas–History.
4. Bellard, Emory. 5. Football coaches–United States–Biography. 6. Football
coaches–United States I. Pickett, Al. II. Title.

GV951.8B45 2010
  796.332092–dc22
  [B]

                                                              2009053445

State House Press
P. O. Box 818 • Buffalo Gap, Texas 79508
325.572.3974 • 325.572.3991 (fax)
www.mcwhiney.org/press

Distributed by Texas A&M University Press Consortium
1.800.826.8911 • www.tamu.edu/press

Printed in the United States of America
ISBN 13: 978-1-933337-41-8 • ISBN-10: 1-933337-41-9
10 9 8 7 6 5 4 3 2 1

Book designed by Rosenbohm Graphic Design

Cover artwork by Robert Winn Hurst
For more information about the artist and to see artworks for sale go to
www.adamnfineartist.com
www.tshof.org

Dedications

Not every coach has the opportunity to live his dream. Not every man gets to create a "life situation" and have a whole lot of people involved with making a dream a reality. I have. During my coaching career, I have served in an assistant's capacity to some outstanding head coaches. Thank you for the experience. I also have headed some great coaching staffs, and to you I say, "Thank you for your great contributions to my coaching career and life."

To the players I have coached, I dedicate this book. You have been my inspiration, my best friends and my drive to success. You have made my life as a coach something unique and rewarding. Coaching you was my dream. Thank you all for making my dream a reality.

—Emory Bellard

To Carole for her love, support and help with the book, and to Emory and Susan Bellard for welcoming me into their home and letting me tell the story of Coach Bellard's remarkable career.

—Al Pickett

Table of Contents

Foreword: Dave Campbell.. ix

Introduction xv

Chapter 1 – Growing Up in Luling.. 1

Chapter 2 – Moving to the Coast.. 9

Chapter 3 – Learning Football.. 19

Chapter 4 – West Texas Football... 29

Chapter 5 – Moving to San Angelo 43

Chapter 6 – Development of the Wishbone 53

Chapter 7 – Rebuilding the Aggies 71

Chapter 8 – Little Bob 99

Chapter 9 – Moving On to Mississippi State................................ 103

Chapter 10 – One More Coaching Stop....................................... 109

Chapter 11 – Organizing Practice 115

Chapter 12 – The Importance of Fullbacks.................................. 121

Chapter 13 – Oh, Those Kickers.. 127

Chapter 14 – Recruiting... 131

Chapter 15 – Wishbone Success 137

Epilogue 141

Index.. 149

Foreword

Few of us who gathered that late September evening in 1968 at Texas Tech's Jones Stadium in Lubbock could have predicted what we were about to see. Coach J. T. King's Red Raiders were about to take on the Texas Longhorns, and most of us expected to see a smashing Longhorn victory.

After all, that was what we had always seen in Lubbock since the Red Raiders had become a part of the Southwest Conference in 1960.

To be sure, the Red Raiders had finally gotten on the scoreboard in 1966 after being shut out on Texas' three previous trips to Lubbock and, yes, they had finally upset Darrell Royal's team the year before in Austin. But this was a different breed of Longhorn, right?

This Longhorn team was strongly favored to win the Southwest Conference championship. It was quarterbacked by senior Bill Bradley, who was called "Super Bill" Bradley for good reason, and it was populated by other outstanding juniors and seniors and also by what some called "the Worster crowd." Rice's Coach Bo Hagan called the previous season's Texas freshmen, led by fullback Steve Worster, the best freshman team "I've ever seen in the Southwest Conference." Now those freshmen were sophomores and raring to go.

In the two teams' respective season debuts, Texas had tied high-scoring and highly-regarded Houston, 20-20. Houston, with its explosive "veer" offense, had started its 1968 season by trouncing Tulane, 54-7. (The previous year, it had defeated such teams as Florida State, 33-13; Michigan State, 37-7; Wake Forest, 50-6; and Mississippi State, 43-6.) Coach Bill Yeoman's Cougars had high octane to spare. For its part, Texas Tech in its debut had only tied Cincinnati, 10-10. So most of those in the Texas Tech press box that night expected to see the Longhorns romp.

Instead we saw the Red Raiders win, 31-22, as safety and punt return standout Larry Alford had the kind of night that would lead him to a place on the 1968 All-Southwest Conference team.

Obviously we were surprised. But we would have been even more surprised if someone had told us what we had just seen. What we had just seen, in the second half of that game, was Texas, Royal and offensive coordinator Emory Bellard introduce a junior quarterback named James Street to the college football world.

Bellard and the Longhorns had found just what they had been missing. They had found an operator with a magical touch who could give their new-fangled "wishbone offense" some real get up and go.

With the 5-11, 180-pound Street at the switchboard, the Longhorns would tie for the conference crown and win the Cotton Bowl game that season and then roar to a perfect season in 1969—one that included a throbbing 15-14 "Big Shootout" victory over Arkansas in a December battle of the unbeatens in Fayetteville (the best college football game I've ever covered)—and then proceed to an almost equally throbbing Cotton Bowl victory over Notre Dame about three weeks later. All that included a national championship personally bestowed on them by President Richard Nixon, who had seen the Fayetteville thriller in person.

The wishbone offense had triumphed over all—Emory Bellard's wishbone offense.

In this excellent book, readers will learn all about the philosophy and the schooling that went into the development of the wishbone, of how it not only led the Longhorns to a pair of national championships (1969 and 1970) but also to a school-record and Southwest Conference-record 30-game winning streak and then accompanied Bellard to a memorable rebuilding job as head coach at Texas A&M and to his Mississippi State's 6-3 victory over Coach Bear Bryant's No. 1-ranked and defending national champion Alabama team in 1980.

I remember vividly some of Emory's more memorable moments at Texas and Texas A&M, but I had forgotten the Mississippi State victory in Jackson over Alabama in 1980. However, reading his thoughts about that victory in his book, I can understand his thinking, which he explains this way:

"Where would that rank among my biggest victories as a coach? Oh, that was big, but you know I've had a lot of really great moments that I have been a part of"—and he cites a Woodsboro game at Ingleside in his first year as a head coach in 1952, the famous victory over Arkansas in 1969, four Southwest Conference titles in a row at Texas, the victory over Notre Dame in the Cotton Bowl to win the national championship.

"When I was at A&M I beat Darrell in his final two years there at Texas; we played LSU 11 times and beat them seven when I was at A&M and Mississippi State. But I don't know if I have been a part of a game that was as emotional as that one against Alabama. After the game, the team had showered and left on the bus to make the drive back to Starkville. I had a car wait for me so I could stay around to do all the media interviews. When I finally got ready to leave after all those interviews, I walked outside and all those Mississippi State fans were still in the stands. It didn't look like anyone had left.

"And in 2007 that game was voted the greatest game in Mississippi State history. They flew a plane over here (to Georgetown), picked up Susan and me and took us to the Alabama-Mississippi State game in Starkville. I got to be part of the opening coin toss, and Mississippi State beat Alabama again that night. That was right after Nick Saban, the new Alabama coach, had just signed that big contract."

Emory's delicious memories? Yes, they're all there in this interesting, largely behind-the-scenes book that will be a fine addition to any football fan's library.

Certainly some of those memories center on Bellard's longtime thoughts about the value of the triple option and his development of what came to be known as the wishbone. It not only paid huge dividends for Texas, but later it did the same for Oklahoma and Alabama and a number of other schools—and it was doing the same for Emory at Texas A&M in 1975 until he lost his quarterback because of an injury just before the undefeated, No. 2-ranked Aggies' showdown in Little Rock against Arkansas. They lost that game to the emotionally supercharged Razorbacks that December afternoon, Arkansas wound up in the Cotton Bowl, and Texas A&M had to settle for a three-way tie for the conference crown and a trip to the Liberty Bowl.

"That was probably the hardest college loss I ever had," says Bellard.

Still, it would be a case of shortchanging him as a top-flight football coach to focus only on his days with the wishbone. He also spent his years at A&M proving himself to be quite a recruiter and builder of programs. The players he recruited at A&M in his years there would fill an Aggie football "Who's Who"—such players as Bubba Bean, Pat Thomas, Ed Simonini, Lester Hayes, Edgar Fields, Tony Franklin, Carl Roaches, George Woodard, and Richard Osborne, and those were just some of them.

And before moving first to the University of Texas and then Texas A&M, Bellard spent fifteen years proving himself to be an outstanding coach in Texas high school football ranks. He began as a head coach at Ingleside, later won outright state championships (one at Breckenridge, one at San Angelo) and tied for another (at Breckenridge) and compiled a splendid record of 136-37-4.

After his years at Texas, Texas A&M and Mississippi State, he retired. But the retirement didn't take. It lasted for two seasons; then, bowing to the pleas of neighbors and friends, he returned to coach the high school team at Spring Westfield for six seasons. While he was there, his teams won a district crown and two regional championships.

This is a man, a Luling native, who truly was born to coach.

If he should ever have been asked to prove his bona fides, that day came when he was hired to coach the Breckenridge Buckaroos. As Bellard remembers it, the school board president told him as he hired him: "We want to go over one more thing with you and make sure you are in complete understanding of what this job is and what it encompasses. We are going to play whatever basketball games we have to play to stay in the Interscholastic League. We are not going to play baseball. You can do what you want with track; you can stress it or not stress it; that is up to you. Our game is football and we are going to play outstanding football, and we want you to understand that."

Bellard certainly understood. In his five years at Breckenridge, the Buckaroos posted a record of 45-14-3; they won a district title, a regional title, a state crown and a share of another.

In all truth, there was something about high school football in that part of West Texas that seemed to bring out the best in both players and coaches. Gordon Wood won two state titles at Stamford and another seven at Brownwood. Art Briles won four championships at Stephenville, and before he got there winning was a foreign word. And Bellard won one crown and shared one at Breckenridge. There must have been something in the water.

For those who like football, West Texas or South Texas or East Texas variety, and high school or major college variety, this book offers much to enjoy.

And I especially enjoyed Bellard's sentiments as expressed on the final pages of the book:

"I have always said that coaching is coaching," he says. "The pros have access to a lot of things. If a player can't cut it, they replace the player. In college, you have players that allow you to win. You recruit them or try to recruit them. If you don't, you are going to have a hard time being successful.

"In high school, you take what you've got and you develop that. You develop a program that feeds what you are trying to do. Maybe the best coaching that is being done anywhere is being done in the high school ranks because you have to play with what you've got."

Playing with what he had, Emory Bellard proved he could win and win big, and how he did it is all here in this book.

—Dave Campbell, editor in chief, *Texas Football* magazine

Introduction

I n a world gone mad for passing, Emory Bellard embraces the wishbone, the eight yards-and-a-cloud-of-Astroturf alignment he invented 24 years ago. Bellard's wishbone chews up yardage at Spring Westfield since 1988, just as it run up big numbers at Texas, Texas A&M and Mississippi State, where he coached from 1966 through 1985, and at countless schools that used it during the ground-based 1970s and '80s.

And it is still misunderstood—and in Bellard's mind, underappreciated.

"I've always felt that people have a misconception that a running touchdown counts six points and a passing touchdown about nine," he said, "and that if you can possibly throw the ball into the end zone, it's much better than running it. I swear to gosh I don't know why."

Listening to Emory Bellard lecture on the wishbone—or on any aspect of Texas football, for that matter—is about as close as anyone can get these days to Moses in coaching shorts.

—David Barron, *Houston Chronicle*, Aug. 23, 1992

Memorial Stadium in Austin, now known as Darrell K. Royal-Memorial Stadium, is home to the University of Texas Longhorns, the second-winningest program in college football. The stadium has been the site of some of the greatest games in college football history, home to national championships.

But one of the defining moments in college football history took place on a lazy summer afternoon in 1968 instead of a day when the stadium was filled with the normal 80,000 screaming fans. It was a day when most UT students were thinking about going for a swim at Barton Springs rather than sitting in Memorial Stadium watching their beloved Longhorns play.

1968, of course, was a tumultuous year in America, with the assassination of Dr. Martin Luther King Jr. in the spring and Bobby Kennedy in June. In the football offices at Texas, however, the focus was on how to reverse three consecutive sub-par seasons. Texas A&M had beaten the Longhorns 10-7 in their annual Thanksgiving Day game in 1967, ending a 6-4 season for Texas.

The 1967 campaign was the first on the Texas staff for Emory Bellard. He said he had turned down college coaching offers every year since his third season at Ingleside High School, as well as his decade-long stints in Breckenridge and San Angelo.

"I didn't want to be an assistant coach," Bellard said. "I wanted to be calling my own shots. The season was over and we won the state championship in San Angelo. I reached a point where that was it. I was either going to stay in high school or I was going to college. I just had to commit myself the rest of the way."

Bellard was obviously one of the hottest high school coaches in Texas. He had had two undefeated seasons at Ingleside and a pair of state titles at Breckenridge and then added the state championship at San Angelo in 1966.

"We won that state championship in San Angelo on my birthday," he recalled. "I was 39 years old that day—Dec. 17."

So Bellard decided to accept Royal's offer and join the University of Texas staff. It was a decision that not only changed the future of Longhorn football and Royal's legendary status with the Burnt Orange faithful but also altered the face of college football itself.

The transformation didn't happen immediately, however.

"Bill Ellington was the freshman coach, and he wanted to know if I would help coach the freshmen," Bellard said. "He asked if I had any experience coaching linemen. Going back to that first year with Henry Armstrong [as an assistant at Alice High School], I have always felt like I was one dang good line coach. I've always had confidence that I could coach linemen and teach them to play football and have them really good. Anyhow, I went up there in the spring. We had spring training, and Mike [Campbell, the defensive coordinator at Texas] asked Darrell if I could come work with the defensive staff and coach the linebackers. He said OK. There weren't any freshmen out there in spring training, so I coached the linebackers in the spring. At the end of spring, Darrell and Mike decided they would put me on the phone in the press box during games. I would coach the linebackers on the varsity and work the phones for Mike on the sidelines for the defense. So I coached with the defensive staff my first year at Texas."

After the disappointing loss to rival Texas A&M at the end of the 1967 season, Royal decided it was time to make some changes.

"After we lost that ballgame to A&M, Darrell and Mike took the team back to Austin," Bellard said. "My wife's folks lived in Navasota, and I was going over to Navasota for Thanksgiving dinner the next day. They had put it off until after the game. After our Thanksgiving dinner, I drove back to Austin, and then the next day I went to Ballinger because there was a linebacker there that we were interested in. I went on out to check on him, and I was in a motel when Darrell called me. He wanted to know if I would take over the offense. I said sure, and he reorganized his staff. We ran the things that I had been running at Breckenridge and San Angelo. We had a good spring training, but the personnel that we had were not players that needed to be out on the flanks or the wings or anything like that. We had [Steve] Worster, [Chris] Gilbert, [Ted] Koy and [Jim] Bertelson. They were all outstanding running backs. That is where the wishbone thing got going."

It wasn't known as the wishbone in June 1968, however. Bellard simply called it his triple option offense. For years, he had been tinkering with the idea, drawing it on graph paper like a high school geometry student.

"I don't know how I got started [drawing on graph paper]," Bellard said. "I just know that the lines may look proper, but it is not proper. You take it out and try it on the field, and it is all together different because it is further to run or it is shorter to run or something. The relative distance is not there. So if you get it down to where these are one-yard squares and then put it all together, you get it all working properly. You've got to be able to do that."

Bellard claimed he first began working on the offense that would become known as the wishbone in 1954.

"We ran it in the original concept in Breckenridge in the state playoffs in 1955," he recalled. "But I always had this feeling there were so many things you could do when you line people up like this. The position of this man to that man to the ball and to the quarterback, to where you were going to ask him to block, it was so relevant that is where we ought to be lined up."

Bellard took the old straight T-formation and moved the fullback closer to the quarterback, right behind him. The halfbacks were moved a step deeper and closer together, lining up five yards behind the offensive guards instead of behind the tackles. The two halfbacks were just two yards are apart.

The move caused the three backs to form a wishbone formation rather than a straight T.

"You don't put people in that obnoxious-looking formation unless there is a reason for it," Bellard said. "Originally we were operating in a blocking scheme that was a little different. Those lines were coordinated, but to do what I wanted to do with the triple option, they weren't. The relative position is the lead blocker's position. I messed with this because you are moving the halfback that is going around that corner out there and moving him two yards toward that corner so he has a running start to get there. You got to have the lead halfback in this position in the wishbone where he can block three points of the defensive structure from that spot. And all of that is coordinated with the read that the quarterback has to make."

So Bellard said he had the idea of what he wanted his triple-option offense to do. But he had to convince Royal.

"After spring training I asked Mike if you can get by with only one split receiver if you have a running play that you need," Bellard continued. "He said yes. It is better with two or more, but I never have liked the idea of just having a guy out there to make the defense make an adjustment. If you are going to drop the defensive back under coverage for him, then you've got to run. Or if he is going to come up here and press the run, you got to be in position to throw the ball. I never did like the concept that the defense can dictate to me what the hell I'm going to do on offense, whether I was going to run or I was going to pass if I wanted to run. I would line up and try to execute the run against the people playing defense against the run. Then if I wanted to throw, I wanted to throw when I wanted to throw, not when they said I could throw. I just didn't like that concept."

Bellard contends that there are three optimums to offensive football. First, he said, you have to have a play where you have a body on a body with a ball carrier running behind it.

"In that situation, you ought to win the fight more times than you lose it; that's for sure," he said. "It is like the old one defender between the dummies and a blocker and the ball carrier back here, then it is two against one."

Bellard's second optimum is a two-on-one situation with an option, which he said is "what the triple option is." The third optimum is getting a one-on-one situation with a pass.

Bellard got everything written up, gave Royal a copy and asked him to look at his offense. It was some concepts and ideas that he thought would be good, Bellard told Royal.

But now he had to demonstrate it on the field. With the Longhorn players having already gone home for the summer, Bellard took a group of seniors who had completed their eligibility but were still around Austin attending summer school and his son Emory Jr. and put together a demonstration for Royal.

"There wasn't a one of them that was involved who was still playing," Bellard said. "I played quarterback to see if I could read the option. I figured that if I could do it, I could darn well teach it to a good athlete."

Bellard said Royal had been running the split-T formation for most of his coaching career, so he understood the concepts that Bellard was touting.

"He liked what he saw," Bellard recalled "Texas had gone through a rough season, but it took a lot of guts on Darrell's part. We put it all together, and then we started having staff meetings about it. I had it all written up, and we were covering everything and looking at all the defenses and certain defensive principles.

"This is based on the certain defensive principles that when you send a receiver deep into the outside zone, you send him straight down the football field. Somebody had to cover him. You can't just let him run down there. Somebody has to acknowledge that you could throw the football to him. That is a principle. When he runs off that line of scrimmage, the ball is going to be thrown deep to him, or whoever is defending the receiver will be a long way from the line of scrimmage. The second man from the defense in that scenario has to be the man that is responsible for the pitch. If the second man takes the pitch, the third man now has to take the quarterback. And where they play the fourth man from the outside dictates how they are going to have to play the fullback from the inside out or the outside in. So those are the basic principles that work for any defense you line up against. If those principles are all there, then the next step is you handling those principles and keeping those principles. That is what the wishbone is."

Thus was born the offense that revolutionized college football. To those who watch the four- and five-wide receiver sets in today's spread football offensive formations, the wishbone may seem like an antiquated offense from another era. But Bellard, who admits that he is still drawing plays on graph paper at age 82, said the wishbone still works today because it is fundamentally sound. The wishbone produced a number of national championships in the late 1960s, 1970s and even into the early 1980s. It was an offense designed by a successful high school coach who moved to the college ranks and revolutionized the game.

This is the story of not only the wishbone offense but also the remarkable life and career of the successful Hall of Fame coach who designed it, as told by Bellard himself, recently named by *Dave Campbell's Texas Football* magazine as one of the most memorable coaches in the last fifty years of Texas football.

It is my thrill to help Coach Bellard tell his story.

—Al Pickett

CHAPTER 1
Growing Up in Luling

My name is Emory Dilworth Bellard. I was the first member of my family to graduate from college. My mother was always very proud of that fact.

My dad was in the oil business, and he had some dealings with a banker in Gonzales, Texas, named Emory Dilworth. The banker told my mom that he hadn't had a son and that if she had a boy and named him Emory, he would put a fund in the bank for me. So she did. There was a lot of camaraderie between my dad and his friend, according to my mom. The banks all went bust after that, so there was no fund. But I still have the name. That is sort of funny. They thought there was going to be something there at some time. Of course, I didn't know anything about it. Anyhow, I didn't get any money, but I am still Emory Dilworth Bellard.

The name wasn't very common at all. It's misspelled with an "e" a lot of times. It's hard to understand how anyone could mispronounce "Emory," but people do all kinds of things with Bellard, which is French. My dad was full-blooded French, and Granddad came from Tours, France. He immigrated through Galveston and migrated up to Beaumont, where he had his homestead. My dad was born in Beaumont. His life was affected by the oil strike (Spindletop, the first major oil strike in Texas) and got into that business. He was a self-made geologist—a very intelligent man. He worked in the oil fields and did all kinds of map work for all kinds of oil companies.

As I said, they mispronounced my last name a lot. I went to Aransas Pass so I could play football my junior year because they didn't have football at Port Aransas. Anyway, that first game at Aransas Pass was against Kingsville, and we went over to Kingsville to play. It was 0-0 going into the fourth quarter. I was playing tailback. In the fourth quarter, I broke loose for about a 30-yard run for a touchdown. I also kicked the extra point, and we beat them 7-0. And man, you talk about being ready for the news reporters. I could hardly wait to call my mother to see if it was all right if I spent the night with one of my friends, Pete Couk.

We played football games in the afternoons back then, so I spent the night with Pete. They were having a class picnic out at the park, and, of course, we were celebrating a win. I wanted to be in Aransas Pass the next day so I could see the newspaper and have everybody read that newspaper about me scoring the touchdown. I could hardly wait.

As it turned out, the newspaper wrote that we beat Kingsville, and all it said was that "Emroy Billiard" scored the winning touchdown and kicked the extra point. You talk about deflating. Man, I'd liked to kill them. My one big moment, and I was so anxious to read that newspaper because I knew it would be in there. But they had my name as "Emroy Billiard" instead of "Emory Bellard." A lot of the boys called me "Billiard" or "Hey, Billiard" the rest of the time I was at Aransas Pass.

Life on Davis Hill

I was born in 1927 in Luling, the watermelon capital of Texas. You are looking at one of the former parade marshals of the Luling Watermelon Festival Parade, which is one of the longest parades in Texas. That was a big moment.

My mother's name was Louie Cass Bellard. She had a man's name, and my dad had a woman's name: Pearl Bellard. Someone would call and ask for Louie Bellard. They would say, "Have your dad to call," and I would say no, that is my mother. Or they would ask for Pearl Bellard and say, "Have your mother call," and I would say that is not my mother—that is my dad.

We lived at what everybody in town called Davis Hill because my mother was a Davis. There was a red clay road that led out of Luling with a couple of hills that were sort of shaped like an "S." There were twelve children in my mother's family, and when they got married, my granddad gave each of them a plot of land to build a house on. At one time, all twelve of those kids had a house within hollering distance of my grandfather's house. All the family was right there. My dad had come to Luling during the big oil strike there. He met and married my mother there in Luling.

Everybody called my granddad Pappy. It was Pappy and Mammy. There was a whole neighborhood of cousins. There were twenty-one first-cousin boys in that neighborhood, and that is not counting the girls. I had two older brothers. One was twelve years older and the other was ten years older than I was.

Football started early in my life because my brothers Norman and Pug were playing high school ball when I was just a little boy. Of course, you could have a heck of a football game with 20 cousins. Every day we would play football or baseball, or we would challenge the other side of town to a football or baseball game. I don't remember any basketball being played there when I was growing up. It was all football and baseball.

Of course, we did other things, too. We would go up in the pasture and find rotten guinea eggs. Those old guineas would lay eggs, and we would choose up sides and have guinea egg fights. There was a clay gravel pit up there, and everybody in that group learned to swim in that old gravel pit.

I remember one time when I was a kid I bought a pair of what I thought were really classy tennis shoes for one dollar. We always had races among the cousins on Davis Hill, and all races, no matter where they started, always went around four trees there. I thought I was really something with my new tennis shoes, but before I got around those four trees in my first race, the soles came off both shoes.

I guess you could look at it like I was awfully darn fast, or maybe those shoes weren't any good.

On Christmas Eve, we would go from this house to that house to another house, and everybody would open their presents and have drinks and stuff at each house. The next day everybody would go to Mammy and Pappy's house, which wasn't but about seventy yards from your house, for Christmas dinner. Pappy was county commissioner of Caldwell County forever. The last time he ran, his campaign poster had a family picture on it and said, "Forty-two reasons why I should be elected county commissioner."

There would have been a time, if some hadn't moved away, that the entire football team in Luling would have been really accented by Davis Hill because every one of my cousins played well. One or two of them went on to college along with myself and played college ball.

Growing up in Luling was about as good as it got. We ran like a pack of dogs. My grandmother never knew who was going to have breakfast at her house. There was never any schedule at her house. When I was a little ol' bitty boy, a lot of times I would get up and tell Momma that I would be going down to Mammy's to eat, and I would run that seventy yards down to my grandmother's and eat down there. She always prepared breakfast for the multitudes.

My mother always prepared breakfast, too, but everybody in the Davis family always had the freedom of going to Mammy's for breakfast if they wanted.

Everybody did at one time or another, and I am sure some of it was by necessity because somebody was gone or wasn't at home to fix breakfast. Mammy always had food, and she had a big table that would seat twelve or fourteen people easily. She never knew, to my knowledge, how many were going to be there; she just always cooked enough for the bunch.

She always had eggs—scrambled, fried or whatever—and she always had sausage. She had a smokehouse and always had sausage out there. We had two uncles who had meat markets, and they would bring her those little pieces of round steak that had been trimmed off of things, and she would have a whole pile of round steak pieces that she would throw in that frying pan. She always had hot and cold cereal, too.

Every morning she prepared pies—fried peach or fried apple or apricot pies with homemade butter or cream that you could put on it. We had cows, so you could have all the whole milk that you could drink. She kept the bottles of milk in the icebox, where they would be cool. You could go in there any time of the day, go in her icebox and get a half pint of milk.

She had a big old crock; she kept a dishcloth on the top of it, and inside she had a big batch of sugar cookies. You could go in there and get a handful of cookies. We would be playing touch football sometimes, and we would say, "Let's go get some milk and cookies." We would run over there, and Mammy would have it ready for us. We would have us some milk and eat a couple of cookies and then go back to playing again. You would put that bottle in the kitchen sink after you drank your milk, and she would wash them out and fill them back up and put them back in the refrigerator. She kept them filled up all the time.

Growing up on Davis Hill was unique.

We went to the picture show on Saturday mornings. We called it "Mickey Mouse" because they had a comedy. Mickey Mouse and Donald Duck were very prominent cartoons at that time. They would also have a continued piece or a serial that would be Flash Gordon or the Lone Ranger or something exciting. It would take you up to a point and then you would have to go back the next week to see what happened after that. They had the comedy and the cowboy picture and then the serial, and you could get all that for about nine cents.

I knew if I could get twenty cents, I could make Saturday in good shape. It cost you nine cents to go to the picture show. Then my uncle had a meat market, and you could go in there and get a ring of sausage for a nickel. They always had a big box of crackers there, and you could get a couple of crackers and a ring of that sausage. Then you could get a cold drink for a dime, and you would go in there and sit at that big table in the back where they barbecued, and they would have knives strapped to the table where you could cut your sausage up. It was the darnedest thing. I needed just twenty cents to make my Saturday.

Tragedy

My dad was in a bad oilfield accident. I think it was in the fall of my fourth-grade year. I'm saying that because the first organized football that they had in Luling was your fourth-grade year, when you could go out for spring training because you were going to be in junior high the next year. The fifth, sixth and seventh grade were junior high, and high school was eighth, ninth, tenth and eleventh grade. By the time I got there, it was twelve grades.

I had been playing football on Davis Hill all the time with my cousins before that, but this was the first time I was able to play organized football. Some of the players in junior high—like Clyde Barrett and Melvin Simmler, who were the starting tailback and fullback on the football team—had to be about 16. They were a good bit older than I was. Of course, they were a couple of grades higher than I was, but at that time lots of students stayed in there longer years. There weren't any rules, so it wasn't uncommon to see a 16-year-old in junior high. Of course, they were out there playing with guys who were 12 years old.

I remember my dad watching me. He came out and watched practice every day because he had gotten out of the hospital and couldn't work. He was broken all to heck. He had his jaw broken and his neck broken. He had to wear a skull cap because his jaw was broken in seven places.

Parts of his jawbone were knocked completely out of his head when he fell back in the rotary on an oil drilling rig. A guy kicked him in the back of his head with the steel-tipped boots that they wore on the drilling rigs, which broke his neck. But that got his head out of the rotary and saved his life. He was in bad shape, though.

My father was a brilliant man. He was the smartest person I've ever known. He could talk about anything. He was really knowledgeable—in the practical sense, too. He could do anything, much unlike me. My middle brother had a feel for doing a lot of those things. He was an electrician in the Navy, so he had those skills with electricity and those systems, but I don't have any of those things because I never had an occasion to be around it. My dad didn't live long enough after we moved to Port Aransas that I even thought about stuff like that.

Dad would come out and watch spring practice. Ernest Webb, who was a lineman, and I were the only fifth-graders who made the junior high team. I don't remember too much about it. The biggest thing I can remember about the first game of the season was riding the bus to go play Gonzales. I don't remember the game or anything about it, but I do remember that everybody had to chew gum. You had to have a big wad of gum in your mouth. I was nervous as I could be anyhow, and my jaws hurt so bad from chewing that gum that I could hardly speak. I was so tired from chewing that darn gum.

I got to play the whole year and got my first letter award. Ernest Webb and I were the only two fifth-graders to letter. My letter sweater was a size 28. It was a green slipover with a white "L" and "junior" on it. I kept that old sweater for a long time. My mother kept them in a chest and thought I might want them someday.

CHAPTER 2
Moving to the Coast

In the spring of my fifth grade year, we moved to Port Aransas. My dad couldn't keep doing what he had been doing in the oil field after his injury. He always loved the coast. I remember going there with him and my uncles and cousins on a couple of occasions to go fishing. He loved the coast, and there probably wasn't too much else he could do where he was. So we sold our house on Davis Hill, moved to Port Aransas and rented a cottage at the Island Cottages.

We went down to the island in a Model A pickup; Mother and Dad rode in the cab, and I rode in the back amidst all the belongings that we had. After we moved, my dad found a boat that needed a new bottom and a complete renovation. He put a new bottom in that boat, got a motor and started taking out fishing parties. He did that until he died. Afterward, my mother ran tourist cottages for a while.

Like I said, Dad could do anything. He got a bamboo needle and made a big mullet net that you could throw with weights on it. You melted lead and put the little balls on the end of it all the way around so you could sink it. You could get mullets and stuff to fish with. My dad and I hunted ducks and went fishing. He operated his boat out of Wilson's Marina—I think that was the name of it. He would take parties out fishing. It was a twenty-four-foot boat with a small seat upfront, an open cockpit and a place for the motor between that and the back seat.

Most of the tourists stayed in the cottages, although there was a hotel, the Tarpon Inn, on the island. President Roosevelt stayed there a lot during his tenure in Washington. He had a yacht and would go offshore. They have quite a lot of memorabilia that they show there from Roosevelt's stays. Every year they had a big Tarpon Rodeo in Aransas, and people would come from all over. Port Aransas used to be a really, really big resort. Padre Island wasn't anything then. There was a little bit of stuff down on the very southern end of Padre Island across from Port Isabel, but most of that island was nothing but 70 miles of sand beach. Nobody ever went over there.

Port Aransas is on the north end of Mustang Island. Aransas Pass is on the mainland. There was a six- to seven-mile causeway from Aransas Pass to Harbor Island, where you would catch the ferry boat to Mustang Island. Harbor Island was where all those ships loaded up with oil. At one time it was the fastest loading operation in the world, especially during the war, filling those big tankers up and getting turned around and back into the Gulf of Mexico, hauling that oil every place in the world. The old causeway had a rail-road track on it, too, where they could bring a train out to Harbor Island.

A ferryboat ran between Mustang Island and Padre Island. There was a cut-through for shrimp boats coming out of Corpus Christi. You would cut through between Padre and Mustang Island, where they had cut a little channel out into the Gulf so those shrimp boats coming out of Ingleside and Corpus wouldn't have to go nineteen miles past Mustang Island before they could get out to the Gulf. They also had a little old hand-drawn ferryboat there; you could drive your truck or car on it and pull yourself across. People went down to Padre Island that way. Some commercial fisherman fished over on Padre Island, but to my knowledge there wasn't any kind of traffic at all that went down to Padre Island for anything other than just to do commercial fishing. Then all of a sudden they got a monstrous highway with bridges and roads, and that is now totally different. But back then, Mustang Island was *the* place to go.

My dad lived only two or three years after we moved to Port Aransas. He never recovered from his injuries. He was a strong man, but it just took his health. He had other complications in his chest that caused him problems. He just never could overcome it. His general health was gone.

When he died, we had a little old cocker spaniel named Beauty. I called it my dog, but it really was Dad's dog. It stayed with Daddy all the time; it would ride with him in the pickup and go on the boat. When my dad died, that little old dog grieved itself to death within two weeks. It just couldn't handle it.

We had also been running the Anglers Court while Dad was doing the boats. After Dad died, my mother continued to run those tourist cottages, which were owned by a fellow named Blunt. I would help her. There's no telling how many thousands of beds I made.

The people wouldn't stay anyplace else because of my mother. They loved her, and she took great care of them. My mother later ran the Lighthouse Cottages, and all the clientele at the Anglers Court just picked up—lock, stock and barrel—and went with her to the Lighthouse Cottages because she would do anything for them.

Some tourists would come down every year. At that time on the island, it was so different. They used to join in on all the island activities. They had an old Woodmen's Hall right next to the Anglers Court, and they would have dances and ice cream parties. All the people on the island would join in, too. So it ended up being like a big family, sort of like living on Davis Hill.

My mother would say, "It is about time for the Joneses from Waco to come in," and sure enough they would be calling to make their reservations. She knew when they would be coming in, and I knew most everybody when they were coming to the island. It really was a family kind of thing.

My mother was the hardest-working person that I have ever known, and she took care of those cottages. I guarantee you there is no way on God's green earth that they could have found any one human being who would consent to do what she did. She was always in there, checking to make sure of this and make sure of that. She was a very responsible person. She was tough as nails and as good as gold at the same time. She lived to be just one month shy of 106.

A desire to play football

When I went to Port Aransas, they didn't play football. They played softball and basketball and had great track teams. We would win the track meet every year. But even track was a lot different then.

One of the events in junior high track was chinning. We won the chinning every year. There was a one-and-a-half-inch pipe on the cross bars underneath the frame of the basketball goal. Mr. Herndon would tell us to chin until we dropped. When the bell rang, we would report to the chinning board and chin and chin until we couldn't. Then we came back after lunch and reported to the chinning board again. That was our training routine. Needless to say, we won first, second and third in chinning every year at the junior high track meet. I know the last year that we chinned, Lindy Laney chinned fifty, Carlos Moore had forty-eight, and I chinned sixty-three. Others would have only twelve or fifteen.

They changed superintendents at Port Aransas, and Joe King came in and brought six-man football during my sophomore year. There was a guy on the island named Tom McNamara, who was a real nice fellow. He was semi-retired, but he had played football at St. Mary's University in San Antonio. He came out and watched the games whenever we would play that six-man football against the little towns around there. We played four or five games, as best I remember. King told me that I ought to transfer to Aransas Pass and play football. He thought I could play football because I was just playing basketball and running track, and he watched all those events. He said, "I'll pay your fees to transfer."

I asked Mother. She said, "Well, if he pays your fee, I can't see any reason why you couldn't if you want to."

I would have to cross the ferryboat and the causeway every day to get to Aransas Pass. The causeway was privately owned by a Mr. Scribner. He said he would give me bus tickets to cross back and forth. He was a real nice man—very religious-minded. He was a big Presbyterian. I was the head of the Sunday School at the Protestant church on the island that was sponsored by the Presbyterian ministry. I was Sunday School superintendent because there weren't any men in the Sunday School or the church—it was just kids and women.

But I only rode the bus once or twice. The only way the bus would have helped me was going over to the mainland, because I never got through in time with my practices to catch the bus back to the island. So for those last two years of high school, I would hitchhike back and forth. Somebody I knew usually was going off the island to the mainland that day, and I would get a ride. Tourists would always give you a ride, too.

Coming back to the island was a different story. The last ferry ran at 10 p.m., and if you didn't get to Harbor Island by 9:45 p.m., you couldn't get to Mustang Island. On occasion I had to stay over at Aransas Pass at a little old hotel over there.

I would go out in the evenings after practice—whether it was football, basketball, track, tennis or anything else that I played—and walk out to the little station where you got on the causeway at Aransas Pass. I would go in and start studying and get my lessons for the next day. Mr. Yeager, who ran the toll station, would ask anybody coming through if this boy could get a ride with them. (If they were in a company car going to the refinery on Harbor Island, they wouldn't let you ride in a company car in case something happened or an accident.)

But I never had any problem getting a ride except for rare occasions in the wintertime. They operated the causeway all night, and Mr. Yeager would always get me a ride. But if you got to Harbor Island too late, you couldn't get home because the ferry had stopped running. You still needed to cross that ship channel. I didn't have a boat, but you didn't need to be running around that ship channel at night anyhow.

I had a little old room there in Aransas Pass at the Jackson Hotel. Mrs. Jackson's son Charlie and I played football and basketball, ran track and all that stuff and went to high school together there. I know she must not have ever rented this room out to anybody else because that was the smallest darn room. It had a half bed in it, and when you got in the room you were practically in the bed. There was no space in it. It had a shower and a commode in it. I kept a change of clothes and a dopp kit (toiletries bag) with toothpaste and all that over there in that old room so that I could have something there if I needed it.

My brothers' influence

Both of my brothers played high school football in Luling. Norman was captain of the team his senior year, and then he went to Westmoreland College in San Antonio, where he played running back and linebacker.

Azel Browning was Norman's coach in high school. They started practice before school started, so he would always come to our house to stay with us for three or four days until school started to give him a chance to find his own apartment. He had real curly hair and a real high voice. He always called me

Chico because in Spanish that means "small," and I was. I'm small now, but I was really small then.

All the football players on the team called me Chico. I was always around the dressing room when Norman was playing. Years later, I would see Coach Browning at Coaches School (Texas High School Coaches Association's annual convention), and he would always holler, "Chico!" I could always recognize his great white hair and real high voice.

My other brother was named Pearl, but everybody called him Pug because he had sort of a pug nose. He joined the Navy early and spent years in the South Pacific. He was supposed to get out of the Navy early the summer after Pearl Harbor. He had been in the South Pacific for more than two years already. About the time he was supposed to get out, the war broke out and he was on the U.S.S. *Marblehead.*

That is a story that is unequaled. He was in the Battle of the Coral Sea, which turned around the naval war in the South Pacific. The American Navy really did a job and won the battles with the Japanese. It was a big deal in the war, and Roosevelt gave a report on the radio. We listened to the radio back then. We hardly turned it off at the house. It would come on automatically in the morning and get me up before I went off to school. My mother would turn it down sometimes, but I would never turn it off.

In the battle that we won decisively, the U.S.S. *Houston* was sunk, and the *Marblehead* was reportedly sunk. The darn hull of that ship had holes blown in it—monstrous holes, as big as that wall over there. But they crippled the ship back into Java and got some repairs, and then they crippled all the way around the world and came back into Boston Harbor on silent radio on Mother's Day that next year. So we thought Pug was dead all that time, but in reality he was alive. He called our mother on Mother's Day and said, "Mom, I'm in Boston in the U.S.A."

Oh, he had some stories to tell. They made a movie called The Story of Dr. Wassell. Gary Cooper played the doctor, who was on the *Marblehead.* When they were in Java, they picked up a bunch of people who were trying to get out of there. It was a pretty complicated story.

Later, the Navy sent Pug back to the Pacific on a destroyer. That was when the kamikaze planes were attacking our ships at the end of the war. His destroyer got hit by kamikaze. He got blown overboard but never got a scratch on him.

Norman was with the Reynolds Company in Brazosport, doing work that was conducive to the war efforts. That's why he didn't go into the service. Of course, I didn't turn 18 until after the war was over. Then when I did go down to take a physical, I couldn't pass because of my eyesight. I got shot in the right eye when I was 7, and I am blind in my right eye. I dropped a BB in the barrel of the gun, and my cousin pulled the trigger.

I don't know how much that bothered me playing athletics. If I ever had any trouble, it was that it was a lot more difficult to catch a ball below my waist. It seemed if it was above my waist, I could catch it and picked it up better. When I played golf, I always used a putter that was like a croquet mallet. I was a darn good putter and could putt it in from about six feet because I could see the line and put it in. Sam Snead started doing it, and then they declared it illegal after he had been doing it for a couple of years on the pro tour. All of a sudden here I am with my croquet putter, and I can't use it anymore. I have been trying since then to get a dominant eye stroke because my right eye was my dominant eye.

Wanting to be a coach

As I mentioned earlier, I was the Sunday School superintendent at the Protestant church at Port Aransas during my sophomore and junior years in high school. Most of the seafarers were Catholic, so there really weren't many Protestants on Mustang Island, and seldom did any men attend the services.

Mr. Scribner, who owned the causeway, was very involved in the Presbyterian church. We would go to different meetings, and there would be a four-county area meeting of the church. They would have a dinner, and they would come out to Port Aransas once a year. We would put out a big seafood feast for everybody.

He told me one time, "Emory, if you will go to Austin College in Sherman, Texas, and study for the ministry, I will pay your tuition. I'll pay all of your expenses. I'll take care of everything you need if you'll go and study to become a minister."

I told him that was a great opportunity for some young man, but I wanted to coach football. I said, "I can touch as many people there as I can the other way." I don't know why, but I was around it a lot and played it. I had always said I was going to coach football; that was what I was going to do. I don't remember doing it because of watching any particular coach; I just loved the game and wanted to coach it.

CHAPTER 3
Learning Football

After playing football for two years at Aransas Pass, I went to the University of Texas to play football in 1945. I was a tailback in the single wing and left halfback in the T-formation. Freshmen were eligible then, and I played two years at Texas.

I was never a great player, but I learned a lot of football at Texas from Coach Dana X. Bible and Coach Blair Cherry. Coach Bible used to talk to us every day before practice for a minimum of at least thirty minutes—sometimes more than that.

At that time, football was a lot different. He had all our offensive plays painted on a blackboard against three different types of defenses that were used at that time. There was the "six-two," which had six people on the line and two people at linebacker. Then there was the "five-three," which had five defensive lineman and three linebackers. The "seven diamond" had seven people on the line and one in the middle.

All those plays were painted on the blackboard, and every day before practice the managers would come in, take the blackboards off the walls around the room, put them in the trailer and haul them out to the practice fields. They put them on tripods behind where the team was going to work. You'd ask, "Coach Bible, what am I supposed to do on that play?" Coach Bible would take you back to the blackboard behind there on those easels and say, "That is you right there."

All these plays had these little terms like sway and snort. Little things like that helped you remember. I loved Coach Bible.

He would also preach the kicking game every day. He said that every close game that will ever be played will be decided by one play from the kicking game. And when you start looking at how many times that occurs, if there has ever been a truer statement about football, I don't know what it is. Every close game that is ever played will be decided by one play from the kicking game. When it gets close, whoever has the best kicking game usually wins it.

Jerome Buxkemper

I broke both bones in my left leg in practice before the A&M game my freshman year. I was running the ball and the guard was in front of me, so I jumped him. I landed on my left foot. As I landed, Peppy Blount, who was from Big Spring, hit me from the outside. All my weight and cleats were in the ground, but my weight was on that one leg, and he came back in from the outside and broke my leg.

I had a cast from my hip to my toes, all the way down. They put steel pins in my leg that stuck out of the cast. Jerome Buxkemper from Ballinger was my roommate. He was a great friend. He had to help me all the time.

The athletic dorm at the University of Texas was being used by the V-12 program. They would go from one university to another, taking courses and giving them their training. They had the athletic dorm, so everybody had to live in boardinghouses around town, wherever you could find a place. Bux and I were sharing a room. Next door and upstairs at this boardinghouse were a couple of other rooms that players shared.

Jerome would have to help me get in and out of a bathtub until I finally could manage that. He also had to help me get to class at times, especially on bad-weather days. I had that cast on for ninety full days.

Bux was coaching in Colorado City later and was going to Coaches School somewhere close to Abilene when he and his wife stopped on the side of the road. I think that was the circumstances. They got hit by a big gas truck, and the thing exploded and killed his wife. Bux was burned everywhere, but he survived. He is a survivor if I have ever seen one. He was burned on his legs and whole body, but not on his face. After he recovered, he was teaching and coaching in Japan at an American school program that they had in foreign countries. While he was in Europe on vacation, he had another really severe car wreck. But he is still kicking and has a good smile on his face. He is a heck of a guy. He lives in Austin now.

Making a move

I transferred to Southwest Texas State in San Marcos after my second year at Texas. I played one year before I hurt my knee, but transferring there turned out to be a good move. Most of the athletes there were majoring in physical education. You had sections on track, basketball, baseball—nearly every sport. You had to demonstrate minimum skills. You had to execute every event in track. Your grade depended on how well you did. Southwest Texas had a really great PE department.

When I graduated, I got a job as an assistant coach in Alice in 1949. Mary Kay and I got married on a Thursday, and I had to report on Sunday to the Corpus Christi Naval Station, where Alice and several other schools were having a training camp together. You could do that in those days. Ox Emerson was the head coach at Alice. That was a blessing because he was a stickler for organization and scouting. I was scouting every week in the Rio Grande Valley. He was a great coach to learn from.

Henry Armstrong was the line coach at Alice. He had played offensive tackle and defensive tackle at Rice under Joe Davis. In those days, you wanted to get a line coach who had played at Rice, so I was with a premier line coach, too. I later coached the offensive line. I always thought I could coach the line from what I learned from Henry Armstrong at Alice or the backs because of the fundamental background I had under Coach Bible and Coach Cherry at Texas.

After that season, Coach Emerson and Henry went to Delmar Junior College in Corpus Christi, and Carl Bage came in as head coach. The superintendent wanted me to stay on as the backfield coach. I said, "Coach Bage may have his own guy he wants to bring in," so I requested that I coach the B-team. We were undefeated. The varsity at Alice, however, was losing game after game. We met on Sundays to watch the Southwest Conference highlights and see what plays we were going to run.

I told Carl that we needed to teach these kids what we wanted them to do. We had just four teams in our district then, and we were 0-6-1 going into district play. He said, "Emory, you take over the offensive line." I was very confident that I could coach the offensive line after working with Henry Armstrong. We were fixing to play Victoria, and Mary Kay was in early labor. I went over to Corpus Christi Ray on Sunday, went to the film room and started studying film. Coach Bage never even looked at film. I took the projector home. I was doing all the things that Coach Emerson did.

On Monday after studying film, I submitted the offense and defense that we needed to run. Coach Bage said to put it in. We beat Victoria soundly, and we dedicated the game to Emory Jr., who was born on Wednesday. We went on to beat Kingsville and Robstown. We had the worst record in the state going into the playoffs at 3-6-1, but we were 3-0 in district. We lost in bi-district. I stayed one more year at Alice, and I coached the backs the next year.

Billy Zimmatore

Billy Zimmatore played quarterback for us. He was a real good athlete. He pitched on a men's fast-pitch softball team. His dad was a retired Texas Leaguer. His right arm was more developed than most kids'. He was also a tremendous punter. In several games, that was a big key.

He was also a talented artist. Every day before practice, he would put some cartoon on the bulletin board. He was really clever. Before the start of his senior season, he got polio and got paralyzed from the neck down. They ran big articles about him in the *Houston Chronicle*. Polio was devastating in those days.

Well, Billy taught himself to paint and write with the pen in his mouth. It was unreal how talented he was. I stayed in touch with him until he died. He would write me wherever I was coaching.

Becoming a head coach

Coach Bage left Alice after that 1951 season, and everybody thought I was going to be the head football coach. When I didn't get the job, Dooley Edwards, the president of the school board, came to me and said: "I think you're too young. I'm responsible for you not getting the job."

Turned out that was the best thing that happened to me. I looked young. I interviewed for a lot of head coaching jobs, and the superintendent would always ask, "How old are you?"

The Ingleside job came open, and they hired me. Coach Emerson was helpful in my getting the job. He was still at Delmar Junior College at the time.

Punk Garrison was the president of the Ingleside school board. His daughter dated Bobby Ray Wright, who was a basketball and tennis player and had big hands. I told him he was going to play quarterback. I think he threw close to 30 touchdown passes in his two-year career.

The year before, Ingleside had gone 2-8. Woodsboro won the district championship and beat the heck out of Ingleside. Both teams had everybody back. We played Woodsboro for the district championship in 1952, and we beat them 34-6. I have never had a team as ready to play as they were for that game. I have been in every kind of game for every kind of championship, but I'm not sure if I have ever seen kids so fired up. I had to walk our kids up and down the sideline just so they could breathe. They were so excited that they were hyperventilating.

Tidehaven beat us 32-28 in bi-district. Freddie Hahn, who was a great tight end for us, dropped a touchdown pass in the end zone; otherwise, we would have won it. But we did so many great things that first year at Ingleside.

The next two years, we won twenty-four in a row and were regional champions back to back. In Class B back then, regional was as far as you could go. We tried to get voted into the district with Hebronville, but they wouldn't let us in. One year at Ingleside, we scored in the first three plays of each game.

We were running the straight T-formation. The last year at Ingleside, I was moving to the concepts of the wishbone. I had a quarterback, Grady Jones, who could throw the ball. He was quick, and he could run. Those were the first concepts of the wishbone.

Robert Haugen

When I was hired at Ingleside, our superintendent, O. T. Blaschke, asked me if it was OK for us to keep Robert Haugen. I didn't know him at the time. He was a good basketball coach, but he had never coached football.

So I closed the gym and took him in there; I put the blocking dummies out and showed him how to block and what to do. I taught him all the things I knew about line play and taught him about coaching football, so to speak. He became a real good football coach, scouting and working with the linemen. Of course, he still had his basketball program.

Ingleside had just a two-man staff. We handled everything—track, football and basketball and helped with everything. Robert became an excellent scout. He would coach the linemen during practice, but he would scout on Fridays, and I would have the game by myself. We had to scout, and he did a real good job with it.

He was more pessimistic about our chances than I ever was. I always felt like we were going to win everything, so it was a good balance because he kept me sort of looking at things a little deeper. He was a fine man and a dear friend, and he did a great job. He always had great basketball teams, too.

Jeffrey Hansen

Nobody has heard of Jeffrey Hansen, but I've always said he may have been as good an athlete as I've ever coached. He moved to Ingleside from Louisiana. They spoke French at home, and he had to struggle with his grades.

I would see him out of the window of my coach's office. He would be out there by himself, and he would run and just spring. He would hit the other foot and he would spring. He was an amazing athlete. When he was in the seventh grade, he could stand under the goal—he was about five-foot-six or five-seven at the time—and just jump straight up and grab the goal. In the high jump, he would just go jump it. I mean that literally. He didn't roll or anything—he would just jump it.

I still remember one night when our junior high was playing Bishop. Ronnie Bull, a great player who went on to Baylor and then into the NFL, played for them. Ingleside kicked off that night, and Bull and that Bishop team just moved down the field—voom, voom, voom—and into the end zone. Then they kicked off, and Jeffrey Hansen ran it back for a touchdown to tie the score, 7-7.

So Ingleside kicked off, and Bishop and Ronnie Bull moved right down the field like a machine and scored again to make it 14-7. They kicked off again, and Hansen ran it back for another touchdown. It was 14-14, and Ingleside hadn't run an offensive play yet. I think it was tied 21-21 at halftime.

By the time Jeffrey got into high school, I was gone to Breckenridge, so he never played for me in high school. I think that first year in high school he suffered a head injury and had to give up football. But he was some athlete.

The last time I saw Jeffrey, they were having a reunion of all those kids at Ingleside right after Susan and I were married in 1994. Here were all those teen-age guys who had gone to gray hair like me. He had come back for the reunion, and I remember him telling me that his daughter was involved in the Olympic trials, so she was apparently a tremendous athlete like him. He had moved to California or somewhere out west. Of course, he never did play high school football, and maybe for one reason or another he never had the opportunity to demonstrate how really good an athlete he was.

They were a great bunch of kids at Ingleside. It was a family community that came about mostly because of the Humble refinery there. It had a pretty good-sized payroll and lots of jobs. Then suddenly they moved that refinery to Baytown and cut way back. After that, most people who lived in Ingleside either had a business there or worked in Corpus Christi. So it became more of a residential area with a bunch of great people. It seemed like they had a cake or pie sale every week I was there. That is an exaggeration, but I could always get a chocolate pie from Mrs. Massey. She was the mother of two boys, John and Billy Fred Massey, who played fullback and halfback for me.

Camp Longhorn

Camp Longhorn originally was a boys' camp. In 1945, I was a freshman at the University of Texas. Tex Robertson was the head swimming coach there at that time; he basically built the swimming program. He had some great swimmers and did a great job. He had been an Olympic swimmer at the University of Michigan.

That spring, he came over to the PE department and asked Shorty Alderson, who ran the men's PE department, if any of the football players would like to work at a summer camp. My roommate and I decided we would like to try it. Of course, Shorty asked all the team members who would like to do it. We went out there for a six-week term in the summer.

There is a state park on the east side of Inks Lake, which is below Buchanan Dam. Camp Longhorn is on the other side of Inks Lake. There were just seven cabins that first year I was there. Tex built the camp for boys, but today it is a boys and girls camp and they have all kinds of stuff. It is a ranch camp. Boy, it has been successful.

I worked there every summer after that. When I was in college, it gave me a summer job so I could save some money. When I got married and started coaching right after that, I would go every summer and take the family out there. It was a great place to work under those circumstances. I later became athletic director out there, too. I worked there every summer as athletic director until I went to San Angelo.

I would go out there and take all my film with me. Everybody watched the films of Breckenridge or Ingleside or even when I was an assistant at Alice. It was a highlight for some of the guys. They would all come over to my cabin. We would put the kids in bed and then watch football films. Many a night there were several counselors assembled to do that. Camp Longhorn was a good job and fit in with my coaching because you had to subsidize your coaching to live.

Weight training

Tex Robertson was the first one to talk to me about a weight-training program. He was ahead of his time. He told me that if I wanted to get ahead in football, I needed to put in a weight program. I said, "Tex, that is taboo."

I took issue with it right away. My knowledge of weight training was typical of coaches back then. I watched those people pick up all that weight, grunt and strain and then put it down. Weightlifters back then were muscle-bound and looked like Charles Atlas. I could see me taking a bunch of kids out there lifting weights. They would all be dead. I was scared of weights, really scared because they were so insecure. Even if you spotted them, what were you going to do? You would have 200 pounds up there above your head, and then what are you going to do? But Tex said we were losing international swimming meets against the Australians because they had a weight program and we didn't.

I didn't have enough sense to jump on Tex's ideas right away. But I always worked with letting the weight of the body be the thing that you are moving and lifting and strengthening the legs with. I just never added the weights on top of them until later, when I was in San Angelo. We chinned, did dips on parallel bars, climbed ropes and all those things. That was pretty much what all coaches were doing. Some had already starting going to the weights, but I didn't because I was still scared of it.

Tex died just a couple of years ago. He was still swimming competitively in those Masters meets up into his 90s, but he said there wasn't much competition in his age group.

CHAPTER 4

West Texas Football

After three years at Ingleside, Breckenridge brought me in for a last visit with the school board before they gave me the job. This was the second trip I made to Breckenridge from Ingleside. That was no small feat. I drove and drove and drove.

The reason they got connected with me was because of Jack Cox, who later ran for governor of Texas in the early 1960s as a Republican and almost won. He lived in Breckenridge and was a great guy. Breckenridge and Breckenridge football was his life along with all the other people in Breckenridge. He got Padre Island a state park and all that business and had a lot to do with its development.

He was living in Corpus Christi at the time, and of course the Ingleside football team got a lot of publicity in the Corpus Christi paper because Ingleside was just across the bay. He had been following us, and one day he came over and asked one of the players where I was. The player pointed me out, and Jack commented how young we all looked. I didn't look very old, I know that. In one sense it was good, and in another it was not worth a dime because people kept thinking you were too young to know what you were doing. I have overcome that in great style, though—looking old, that is.

"Coach Bellard," he said, "I'm Jack Cox. I was born and raised in Breckenridge." Anyone who coached knew about high school football and where Breckenridge was and what an outstanding program it had. He wanted to know if I would be interested in the head coaching job at Breckenridge. He had been following Ingleside in the paper; he was constantly in touch with the people back in Breckenridge and went back to games all the time and all that business.

I remember one time we were fixing to play Graham; they had beaten Comanche something like 90-0 that year and had a great football team. I caught Jack painting the words "another Comanche" on our field house in red and blue lettering. He was a character. He was laughing and said he was supposed to sneak in and sneak out, saying Graham had done it.

Anyway, Jack was primarily responsible for how I got connected with the Breckenridge job. I interviewed in the normal way and had gone through the process; then they called and said they wanted me to come back one more time. So I got in my car and took off again for Breckenridge. When I got there, the school board president said: "We want to go over one more thing with you and make sure you are in complete understanding of what this job is and what it encompasses. We are going to play whatever basketball games we have to play to stay in the Interscholastic League. We are not going to play baseball. You can do what you want with track; you can stress it or not stress it; that is up to you. Our game is football, and we are going to play outstanding football, and we want you to understand that."

That was about as blunt as you can get it. I said: "You're talking my way. Football is my game, too." It was a great place to coach.

We worked out early in the morning during two-a-days before school started. Several of the kids lived out of town. Coaches drove out in the country and picked up players and took them home in the afternoon. We worked hard. We weren't going to lose a player because he didn't have a way to get to school and back out. The bus wasn't on the same schedule as the players were, so there was no other way to get them home. So every night we would spread out over the county—it was a county school—and we would take the kids home to the far exchanges of the county, wherever it was.

Emory Bellard
(Photo provided by Emory Bellard)

You could do a lot of things then that you can't do anymore. We would have breakfast in the cafeteria, which was legal. We had to pick them up at 5 in the morning. We would work them out and then go in and have breakfast. Some of those kids wouldn't have had anything to eat. We had good breakfasts. I have always been a breakfast man.

We would start practice at six o'clock in the morning of two-a-days, when it was as cool as we could get it. A bunch of people would be in the stands at 6 a.m., watching the Buckaroos work out. They were very knowledgeable about football. They knew what it takes and when it was not going right and when it was. They were tough in a way, but not too tough. It was great.

Joe Kerbel and Cooper Robbins had both won state championships at Breckenridge before I got there. In fact, in the first seven years that there was a 3A division, I think Breckenridge won a state championship five of those years. Robbins went on to Odessa and Kerbel went to Amarillo.

Success in Breckenridge

That first year in Breckenridge, in 1955, we lost to Stamford 21-14 in the quarterfinals. Gordon Wood was at Stamford, and he did a good job of coaching. Mike McClellan was just out of this world, Bob Harrison is in the Big Country Athletic Hall of Fame, and Gordon did a good job of coaching. (McClellan and Harrison both went on to play at Oklahoma, and Wood became the winningest high school coach in Texas.) They were a good outfit, a solid outfit. We had a chance to win that game, but they stole the ball from Bennett Watts, our quarterback, right down on the goal line. They went on to the state championship. That was Gordon's first of nine state championships.

The next year, 1956, was the toughest season I had as a coach. We didn't have any juniors and seniors that season. Bobby Goswick broke three bones in his right hand. We went 4-6, and that was the only losing season Breckenridge ever had.

In 1957, we won the district championship again, and Sweetwater beat us in the quarterfinals. Sweetwater went on to play for the state championship, but they didn't win it—they lost to Nederland in the finals.

The next year, in 1958, we played Sweetwater for bi-district. We were ranked first and second in the state. We played in Sweetwater at the Mustang Bowl, and we beat them 16-14. That was a tough football game. We had a couple of two-point plays in case we needed them. As it turned out, we made both of those two-point plays, and we needed them. We won because we converted them. Sweetwater was a big, strong power football team. We had beaten them earlier (35-20 in the opening game of the season). We also beat Wichita Falls (26-22) that year, and they won state in Class 4A.

After our bi-district win over Sweetwater, we beat Andrews (44-0) and McKinney (26-7) to reach the Class 3A state championship game against Kingsville. Bill Creagh, who wrote for the *Breckenridge American*, wrote a little book after the season with a game-by-game description of that 1958 season.

■ ■ ■

Pete Shotwell burned his name into Buckaroo history on a snow-covered park at Waco in 1929 when his Breckenridge ball club tied Port Arthur 0-0 in the state finals. The 1951 Buckaroos immortalized Cooper Robbins by bumping Temple 20 to 14 in 1951 for an AAA state championship. Breckenridge's 1952 and '54 clubs boosted Split-T specialist Joe Kerbel into the Sainted Circle by grabbing two state championships. Kerbel's '52 club clipped Temple 28 to 20 and his '54 group trimmed Port Neches 20 to 7. In meeting Kingsville, Bellard was presented his opportunity to carve his name into Buckaroo immortality.

—Bill Creagh, *Breckenridge American,* December 1958

■ ■ ■

We won the coin toss, so Kingsville had to come to Breckenridge. We beat Kingsville 42-14, which I think was the highest score that anyone had made in a state championship game at that time. We went 13-1 that season. Our only loss was to Abilene. They had a pretty fair country outfit themselves. But we had a great football team, a bunch of kids who could really play.

When I was in Ingleside, Jake Trussell, who lived in Kingsville and wrote for the newspaper there, had a Thursday-night radio show. He was always making predictions on the upcoming games. We won 24 straight football games at Inlgeside, and about three-fourths of the time he predicted that we were going to get beat.

After we beat Kingsville for the state championship, he wrote the danged-est article I've ever read. It was complimentary about the football but not about Breckenridge.

■ ■ ■

For years I'd heard of Breckenridge and its high school football team, but not until Saturday did I learn the facts of life. I finally made the pilgrimage to Breckenridge, and as a long-timer writer on the subject of high school football, I think "pilgrimage" is the right word to use. No football fan will ever know how great high school football can be played until he's seen the Breckenridge Buckaroos perform on their home field.

After the Kingsville Brahmas beat massive Cleburne, I couldn't imagine Breckenridge being any better than that giant Cleburne team. So I picked Kingsville to knock off Breckenridge 24 to 20. It was a classic example of ignorance being bliss.

I felt sure of my prediction until the fans' bus upon which I rode to the game came in sight of Breckenridge. But as I saw Breckenridge as the bus approached the town and then drove through it, I became vaguely uneasy. By the time I had gotten out of the bus and entered the Buckaroos' stadium, and climbed to the press box, I had a deep down aching feeling that Kingsville was going to get the axe.

Breckenridge Saturday was the meanest, toughest, rawest, ugliest looking town I have ever seen—and it had a football team to match. The comparatively small town was sitting on barren, wind-swept, frost-bitten, Northwest Texas hills. There wasn't a speck of green in sight anywhere. Separate portions of the town actually looked like sets out of "Gunsmoke."

As our bus wheeled through the streets of this God forsaken-looking community, we noticed that there were no automobiles, pedestrians or stragglers on the streets. Everything appeared to be closed down. Breckenridge actually looked like a ghost town.

"Where is everybody?" someone asked.

A few minutes later we discovered the answer to that question. They were all at the football stadium, preparing to watch another slaughter.

Once again, I used a word advisedly. "Slaughter" is the right verb-adjective to describe the way Breckenridge dismembers a visiting football team. And the staging is absolutely perfect.

The Breckenridge football stadium looks like a combination rodeo chute-slaughter pen-concentration camp. Old, rough, wooden bleachers surround the playing field on three sides. The football field itself doesn't have a single blade of grass on it. The softest thing on that gridiron Saturday was the line markings. It was as barren, and almost as hard, as if the two teams had been playing on a tennis court.

The football field is surrounded by a concentration camp-type fence, right off the end of the field, and immediately behind the fence the thousands of screaming Breckenridge fans roar their approval of the Buckaroos and their disapproval of the visiting club. No wonder the Buckaroos are almost invincible at home. The opposition is intimidated before a single play is ever run.

If I was a coach and took a team into Breckenridge seriously expecting to win, I wouldn't step into that stadium without submachine guns and hand grenades. The implication automatically is that if you ever win a game there, you'll have to fight your way out of town.

On the field of play itself, the Buckaroos present the quickest, fastest, hardest-hitting high school team you will ever see! The secret of their success is mainly two-fold: A great tradition of being a football town and team speed as an eleven-man unit that is absolutely amazing.

On their home field, the Buckaroos play as if they know that, if they lose, they will each and every one be run out of town. Those Bucks are not just playing football. They're fighting for a happy home and the right to walk down the streets of their own city.

Their speed as a team is breath taking. One Kingsville fan came through with the best description of the way the Bucks operate. Said this fan, "They come up to the scrimmage line, squat down, and then took off like a covey of quail."

Actually, the Buckaroos moved quicker erecting their offensive plays than any team I have ever seen, high school, college, or pro. They waste no time at the scrimmage line. They work the plays through the middle so fast that neither the fans nor the opposition know what's happening until the runner is into the secondary.

On the field of play, the Buckaroos are good sports. They didn't try "to get" Kingsville's colored athletes, as had been rumored in advance. They simply knock you into the middle of next week, then run back to the huddle to call the next play. They're too great a team to waste time on dirty football.

After it was all over Saturday, my reaction was as follows. I knew I'd finally seen the greatest in high school football. But if I had to live in Breckenridge to be state champions, I'd just stay in Kingsville and be runners-up.

For one of the reasons the Breckenridge boys play great football is because of the simple and obvious fact that they have nothing else to do. The isolated, forlorn, and desolate cowtown-oiltown sits alone and overlooked by the rest of civilization until somebody mentions the game of high school football!

—Jake Trussell, *The Kingsville Record,* December 24, 1958

Bill Creagh wrote an article for the *Breckenridge American* responding to that article and sent it to the Kingsville paper. Jake sent another one back. I don't know how many thousands of newspapers they sold as a result. It was really complimentary in a way, but it had a lot of tongue-in-cheek stuff in it.

Dickie Rodgers was our fullback on the 1958 team. Jerry Gibson was our quarterback, and Joe Ed Pesch and Jimmo Wilson were halfbacks. Bobby Walker ran a double reverse and broke for a twenty-five-yard touchdown against Sweetwater. Joe Ed Pesch, Larry Kimberlin, Charles Huddleston, W. H. Roberts, Dickie Rodgers, Joe Crousen, Larry Parker and Jerry Gibson were all-staters that year.

Bill Creagh wrote a book about that season that was dedicated to P. W. "Trey" Pitzer III. Bill Pitzer was a great man and on the school board at that time. Trey, his son, died on the field on October 16, 1958. He was in junior high at the time. He was a fine young man. It nearly killed everyone there. He just laid down; he was doing a tackling drill, but the doctor said that wasn't what killed him—it was an aneurysm. He could have turned over in bed and had it.

Mr. Buckaroo

When we played Graham in my first year at Breckenridge, their quarter back was Sonny Gibbs, who went on to TCU. They also had a great fullback named Mike Dowdie, who ran a nine-five hundred and weighed about 215. He was a stud and went to Texas.

We had a kid named Buddy Hamilton who weighed about 145 pounds. Graham played a really extreme wide offensive line in their offense, and if you didn't watch yourself, you would line yourself up out of the play. For this game, we stacked our linebackers in and keyed the front linebacker on the fullback. Buddy was normally a secondary guy, but in this particular game he was playing up there at linebacker at only 145 or 150 pounds.

Buddy would hit their fullback because he was always the first man in whatever play they were executing. He just kept hitting that son-of-a-buck. Then in the middle of the fourth quarter, he tackled him one more time, and Buddy rolled over and stayed on the field. I went out there to check on him, and he said: "Coach, that's all. I'm shot."

I asked him where he was hurt. "I'm not hurt," he said. "I don't have anything left."

After the game, his mother told me that before he left the house for the game that night, he told her: "I am going to give it everything, every ounce that I got tonight, I promise you that."

You see guys run toward the finish line in track and collapse in fatigue. But how many times have you seen that on the football field? I have been out there with a lot of great efforts, but that was the first time I ever witnessed that in football by any players. They put a big picture of Buddy in the field house, and he got the title of "Mr. Buckaroo." His two front teeth were out, and you could mash his nose down because it was broken. But he was tough.

Taking a big bite

Joe Crousen, who played for me at Breckenridge, later coached for me at Mississippi State. I will never forget a story about Joe.

We were playing Brownwood in 1958, the year we won the state championship. Brownwood's biggest threat that year was dropping their tight end back as a wingback, bringing him in motion, pitching the ball to him and letting him throw. He was a big old boy, and he could throw that ball out of sight. They used that quite a lot and pitched it back to him and let him throw deep. They had good receivers, and they kept throwing it. We would break it up at the last minute. I think they completed only one of them, but we knew they were going to do it. It just always got down to whether you made the defensive play and knocked the ball away.

It really wasn't that big of a deal to cover it as long as he stayed in the game. But they were a threat and could score a touchdown on you real quick because this guy could throw it so darn far. We were jumping for the ball down there, but we were winning most of those fights.

Offensively, we were running that football and we were moving that ball and just busting holes in it, but we weren't getting in the darn end zone. We'd get down there and screw up somehow. We'd jump offside or do something. I was getting frustrated as heck.

We started another drive and had gone the length of the field and were down around the twenty-yard line. All of our sudden our huddle just busts open and everybody is dying laughing. I called timeout and called Jerry Gibson, our quarterback, over to the sideline. "What in the world is going on out there? We just got a five-yard penalty because we were late getting the play off."

"Coach, you're not going to believe this," he said.

Jerry said that Crousen, who was our right guard, was the first one back in the huddle after the play. Joe said, "I just bit the living daylights out of that old boy." Then Larry Kimberlin, our left guard, came back to the huddle. He said, "That sorry son-of-a-gun bit the hell out of me."

Joe had bitten Larry on the leg, thinking he was a Brownwood player. And the huddle just broke open. Even though I was frustrated and we had a five-yard delay-of-game penalty, I just broke down and laughed, too.

Winning it again

We won a second straight state championship in 1959. Actually, we tied Cleburne in the state championship game.

We were up by two points and then scored a touchdown to go up by eight, 20-12. If I would have kicked the extra point, we would have had too many points for them to make up in one single score. Of course, we didn't have any guarantee that we would make the kick; we didn't have a good kicker. So I decided to go for two, and we failed to score. It was my mistake.

Cleburne completed a pass for a touchdown and then completed another pass for the extra points at the very end of the game to tie us, 20-20. Their kids were thrilled, and our kids were bawling. That Cleburne team had David McWilliams (who went on to play and coach at the University of Texas) as a center and linebacker. Timmy Doerr on that Cleburne team also went on to play and coach at UT.

In the first series of plays from scrimmage in that game, Dickie Rodgers, our fullback and also our starting linebacker, took the ball 39 yards on his first carry. When they tackled him, he broke his collarbone, and that was all for him.

We sent in our backup fullback Travis Gandy to replace him. Travis was a little-bitty guy. He had sort of a bad knee to start with, and he got it hurt again in his first series. So we had a kid named Poston who was a freshman on the B-team. We suited up all the B-team kids for the playoff games that year because they had finished their season and we needed all the players we had. He played nearly all of that game except the first two or three plays.

There were a lot of good football players who were on both state championship teams, including quarterback Jerry Gibson. We had only nineteen players on that team, but one example of the type of players we had was Jimmy Wright. He was the backup quarterback and played in the defensive secondary, but he was also one of the bigger players on our squad. He had played quarterback and free safety the year before, and he had been a quarterback his entire career.

I talked to Jimmy about moving to the line, and he became an offensive tackle and played defensive tackle. Jerry was really a natural quarterback. He was smaller than Jimmy, but he had a feel for the game and the things we did. So Jimmy moved to offensive and defensive tackle that season and did a heck of a job. We just didn't have enough people, so we had to get our best players on the field.

That 1959 team was a very good one. We tied Wichita Falls that year, and our only loss was against Abilene. I think that was the only time we played Abilene in Breckenridge. We always went to Abilene, and we always went to Wichita Falls (both larger-classification schools that won a combined four state championships in the 1950s). That was tough sledding.

Although Jerry was our quarterback, Jimmy threw a touchdown pass from the guard position in that game against Abilene. It was a legal execution of getting the ball to the guard, and then the guard stepping back and throwing the football. We had everybody on the team hollering fumble and two or three on the line of scrimmage diving on the ground. Jerry took it, rolled back and then handed it to Jimmy. Jack Stephens, our end, was running down the field, and Jimmy threw it to him for a touchdown.

Winning coin tosses

We played that game against Cleburne in Breckenridge. That was the second year in a row that we won the coin toss and got to play the state championship game at home in Buckaroo Stadium.

But I was the world's worst at flipping the coin. I forget how many in a row I lost for a while at both Ingleside and Breckenridge. The players would tell me, "Coach, don't you flip the coin," because I would lose every time we flipped. John Culwell, who was superintendent of schools in Breckenridge, eventually said: "Give me that coin; I'll flip it and I'll win."

And he would. He won a couple of those. I wouldn't even mess with that coin. If you flipped it, it had to hit the ceiling and land on the floor. They got in so many discussions. There were so many rules. I've seen coins bounce on couches and stuff and not even come up heads or tails. I've seen so many things happen. Now they go even or odd on ZIP codes in the coaches guide. They do things so differently now, but that was a really fun era.

CHAPTER 5

Moving to San Angelo

After the 1959 season, I was offered the offensive coordinator's job at Texas A&M. When we were practicing in the playoffs, I kept seeing guys up in the stands. People scouted you from everywhere in the world. You couldn't just go out and work out without the possibility of somebody out there scouting you. That was true all over West Texas.

One day these two guys were up in the stands, and the next day they were up in the stands again. Nobody recognized them, so I sent the manager over there to find out who in the heck they were. It was a fellow named Pete Peterson from Fort Worth and one of the assistant coaches, I guess—anyway, someone connected with A&M. He was a former A&M student, anyhow, but when I asked who they were, they said: "Coach, we don't want to bother you." They said they were just watching and making a coaching assessment up there about how our practices were organized and how we were organized. They said, "We'll talk to you after your final game."

And they did. I was offered the offensive coordinator's position at A&M. The head coach, Jim Myers, was in trouble. They weren't playing good, and they weren't getting any better, I guess. I went down there and visited with them. It was a great setup and opportunity for me, other than it was that assistant coaching thing. I sure didn't want to be an assistant, and I darn sure didn't want to be an assistant coach to a guy who wasn't pretty solid in his position. I worked too long, and I never would forget that experience I had in Alice.

I was also offered the head coaching job at San Angelo, so I decided to go to San Angelo and then take a chance on getting a college job later. I was there for seven years, from 1960 to 1966.

We were very mediocre the first year, but we won the district championship the second year. Wichita Falls, the eventual state champion, beat us in the semifinals. They had a great ball club. Joe Golding, the coach at Wichita Falls, was a good friend. We played them when I was at Breckenridge. They ran the single wing, but then they started incorporating a bunch of things in their offense that we had used when we were playing them. So basically they were running our offense.

Getting stronger

As I said earlier, I always worked with letting the weight of the body be the thing that you are moving and lifting and strengthening the legs with. We did parallel bars and shinnied up a rope, did chin-ups and those kinds of things. We also did agility drills. That was the program we had. Those kids always had some innate strength.

When I got to San Angelo, the first thing I did was have the rope bracket and the parallel and chin-up bars set up the way they should be. I would take those kids out and put them up on the rope, and they would just hang there. You would put them on the parallel bars, and I was afraid somebody was going to tear both shoulders up. They would start out and they would just go all the way through the bars. They couldn't chin, either. So that was the first time I ever put in a weight program; those kids were so weak that they just couldn't do those things. We started that weight program, and the next year we played good.

There was no sense in trying to improve their strength when they couldn't even support their own body strength. James Brown, who was involved in the gymnastics program in San Angelo, was from Breckenridge; he tried all the time to get me to put in a weight program at Breckenridge. He was a little short guy who lifted weights all the time. He was real muscled up, and I kept telling him my objections to it. The big thing was watching those kids wavering around with those 200-pound weights on their shoulders. It was just frightening to me.

But I called James Brown, because he was working there in San Angelo, and said we were going to design a weight-lifting rack, and we did. It would slide up and down poles, and we would put pegs in them so the weights wouldn't go any lower. We had it to where we could put a peg through those holes, and that was anchored at the top and at the bottom so there wasn't any way there could be any swaying or getting over-balanced. The only way it could go was straight up and straight down. I felt comfortable with that. We had it where you could put these keys in the holes and that weight couldn't go down any farther, whether it slipped or you slipped. I designed the thing or told him what I wanted on it and how to do it, and he did it and then sold them.

Those kids were really weak, but we got that done and they could work out. I didn't mind them being in there working out by themselves because they had all the safety factors in there. It couldn't fall on them at any time because of the way it was designed.

We won the district in 1961. In fact, we won the district four times in the seven years we were there in San Angelo. That was the heyday of the Little

Southwest Conference. It was the best district in the state at that time. Houston and some of those other areas hadn't come on yet. Later they started putting together programs that would give them the kind of edge they needed.

In 1965, Odessa Permian beat us 8-7. We scored first to take a 7-0 lead. They came down and scored and went for two. The thing that really killed me was that we defended that particular play every day in spring practice. That was a play that everybody runs—the whole universe. The kicker comes out; the holder takes the snap and rolls out into the flat and throws a pass. It is a universal play. We had special plays, and they had special plays that they used. Every day we had time set aside for that—I mean every day—defending against the two-point play. When we would run those plays at our defense, we would stop them. But they threw the perfect pass. Our kid was out in the flat and knew it was coming. They executed it real good, and we just couldn't—or didn't—defend it. Anyway, we lost 8-7, and then Permian went on and won the state championship.

A title for my birthday

The next year, 1966, it was a struggle just to get out of district. Just one team went to the playoffs in those days. We beat Abilene Cooper 20-7 to give Cooper its only loss. That was the year that Jack Mildren (who became Oklahoma's first wishbone quarterback) and all that crew at Cooper were juniors. They went to the state finals the next year in 1967.

We lost to Permian, 12-6. Cooper beat Permian, 28-17, and Permian tied Abilene High, 10-10. So Permian had a loss and a tie. Cooper and San Angelo each had just one loss, but we went to the playoffs because we beat Cooper.

We decided to change our uniforms that year. San Angelo had always emphasized blue in its uniform, but we went to an orange uniform—an orange jersey with blue stripes, orange pants and orange helmets. Bob Milburn, who was the sports editor of the *San Angelo Standard Times,* started calling us the

"Angry Orange," and *Orange Blossom Special* became our official song. When we played Amarillo Tascosa in the quarterfinals, our booster club chartered a train to take fans from San Angelo to Amarillo. They said they played *Orange Blossom Special* all the way up there.

San Angelo beat Spring Branch to win the state championship in Austin on my birthday. I was 39 years old that day—December 17, 1966.

■ ■ ■

AUSTIN – Awesome San Angelo almost counted its Christmas blessings too early here Saturday afternoon, but the "Angry Orange" from West Texas put together three ball control touchdown drives and beat Spring Branch to the win, 21-12, in the 1966 Class AAAA high school football championship round.

The highly favored Bobcats uncorked scoring marches of 65 and 61 yards in the first half, using up 25 plays and 12:27 of the Memorial Stadium scoreboard clock, to grab a 14-0 intermission lead.

But Donnie Wigginton caught the Bobcats napping twice in the fourth quarter and belied them with two quick touchdown passing strikes and almost, but not quite, pulled the Bruins up even.

The big play in the final, viewed by 20,000 in perfect football weather, came late in the fourth period when the Bobcats, leading 14-7 and having trouble with the upset-bound Bears, struck through the air for 40 yards to set up the touchdown that iced it away.

Facing third and needing five, San Angelo quarterback Gary Mullins completed his only pass of the afternoon, a 40-yard toss to Mark Dove that carried to the Bear 10.

Four plays later, Mullins muscled his way over from the one and the Bobcats put it out of reach at 21-7 with only 2:08 left.

Wigginton, thanks to an unbelievable catch by Red Johnson, got Spring Branch one more TD, but it was too late.

—Bill McMurray, *Houston Chronicle*, December 18, 1966

■ ■ ■

■ ■ ■

In Care Of: Coach Emory Bellard, San Anglo Central High

Congratulations to the Angry Orange Bob Cats on your winning of the AAAA state football championship. Having competed with the largest high school in our great state you have won the highest football victory in Texas. Your teamwork, sportsmanship, athletic skills and spirit have been magnificent. I join our many fans in cheering your achievement. May this laurel wreath of victory rest easy upon your brow.

—U. S. Senator Ralph W. Yarborough, Western Union telegram, December 19, 1966

■ ■ ■

We had reservations at a steakhouse in Austin after the game. After we won the state championship, we went there for dinner. The cheerleaders and some other people joined us. I hadn't gotten my steak yet, and the waitress said they had given out all the steaks we had ordered. Our superintendent told her, "You bring out some more steaks, and you keep bringing them out until we say stop." I was never so proud of a superintendent. For once, he didn't worry about how much something cost. We went back to San Angelo that night after dinner. As soon as we got close enough to pick up the San Angelo radio station, we started listening to it on the bus. They were playing *Orange Blossom Special.* As we got closer to town, there were cars all along the highway in the ditches, blowing their horns when the buses went by. Then the cars would join in the caravan. When we got into San Angelo, the buses went through the residential areas of town. The radio station would report where the buses were, and people would come out in their yards to cheer us. We were listening to the radio station in the buses at the same time. We ended up at the stadium. They turned the lights on, and we had the darndest pep rally you ever saw. It was a night to remember.

Remembering Wayne Dacy

My second year at San Angelo in 1961, we were playing Permian. They had Mike Love. He was a big running back and also their kickoff man. Everybody in football has run a kickoff return where you send the middle man with the front five at the kicker to make him go one way or another to rattle him. It used to be run consistently.

I never did do it because I never felt we had the person who could hit the guy, and it was a waste of somebody to let him go by while he was up there screwing around. But we had a guy named Wayne Dacy. He was a senior that year and was the middle man on our kickoff return. Someone was running that on a film that we were looking at, and I said, "I think we will go ahead and put that in," because I always liked the return factor because of the middle man and all that coverage possible to spook the kicker.

Anyhow, we did it and Dacy became a marked human being. He was unreal. Whenever Dacy would go after the kicker, he would hit him right between the numbers. It was unbelievable.

The next week we played Midland Lee, and they had a kicker who went on to the University of Oklahoma. He was a fine football player. There wasn't any attempt at trying to hurt anybody. That wasn't the intent. But all of a sudden we started doing something and we had somebody that could do it, and nobody else had anyone who could do it. He hit that Midland Lee player right between the numbers. The crowd was booing.

Then we played Abilene; their kickoff man was Jack Middlebrooks, who was their great running back. Dacy parked that son-of-a-gun, and he was so busy dodging Dacy that they had no kickoff game. Every time we put Dacy out there to block the kickoff man, he would accomplish it. Lots of teams in the country were using that exact same return, but they didn't have a Wayne Dacy. We had a good kicking team, but it wasn't just because of that. It was just one of those things that happened.

There was some bad blood for a while because we made the return up the middle. We hit the kicker and cross-blocked and came up the middle. We made some pretty good returns. We didn't make any touchdowns on them. It was just a simple fact that everybody used that return at one time or another, but nobody had a Wayne Dacy. I tried it a bunch of times before and after, but I never had a Wayne Dacy except that year. That son-of-a-gun would hit you.

Leaving the high school ranks

What had been considered more or less a routine San Angelo School Board meeting tonight has now taken on the aspect of an all-important session for the city's sports fans.

Out of the meeting will come the decision of head football coach and athletic director Emory Bellard as to whether he will continue as the local helm or turn his talents to Austin as a member of the Texas University coaching staff of Darrell Royal.

Bellard, current president of the Texas Coaching Association who led the Central High Bobcats to the pinnacle of Texas schoolboy football last fall with a state Class AAAA championship, confirmed Wednesday that he had received a tempting offer from Royal and was seriously considering accepting it. He said he probably would not make a decision until Friday, after the school board has an opportunity to act on his request for a salary raise.

Supt. G.B. Wadzeck said Bellard's contract, which still has over a year to run, to June 1968, would be discussed. He said he felt certain the board would vote the 39-year-old coach a new contract calling for a "substantial raise that would make him the highest-paid coach in District 2-4A, should he elect to remain here."

Wadzeck said he had talked to Bellard Wednesday afternoon and had invited the coach to appear before the board if he so desired.

Bellard, who came here in 1960 after winning a state Class AAA title at Breckenridge while sharing another with Cleburne, started out here at $8,500. He is now making around the $11,000 mark for his dual duties as athletic director and head coach.

Although the two have been friends a long time, the first contact between Royal and Bellard in regard to a job at Texas was made last Saturday.

The Bobcat coach said the move to Austin, if he makes it, would be strictly for economic reasons now and in the future, that he thought the San Angelo position was the finest high school coaching spot in Texas.

"I have turned down offers of lesser jobs at more pay in the past," Bellard said, "but I have three children I am going to have to provide an education for. I have to think of this."

The Bellards have a son, Emory Jr., who is a Central sophomore, a daughter Debra in Lee Junior High and a son Robert, who is pre-school age.

—*San Angelo Standard Times,* January 1967

■ ■ ■

Every year after my third year at Ingleside, and every year that I was at Breckenridge and San Angelo, I was offered an assistant coaching job in college. Like I said, I didn't want to be an assistant coach. I wanted to be calling my own shots. The season was over, and we won the state championship in San Angelo, and I had reached a point where that was it. I was either going to stay in high school or go to college. This was all there was to it.

After we beat Amarillo Tascosa, Darrell Royal called me the following week and said he wanted to talk to me at the end of the season. I don't think I would have gone anywhere else but the University of Texas at that time. I felt like Darrell was stable in his position, and I had to decide if I wanted to go on to the college level or if I was going to stay in high school. I just had to commit myself the rest of the way.

■ ■ ■

AUSTIN, Texas – Emory Bellard, 1966 Class AAAA state championship coach at San Angelo High School, has joined the football coaching staff at the University of Texas.

Darrell Royal, UT athletic director and head coach, completed his staff Thursday with the hiring of Bellard, whose teams in 15 years won 11 district and three state championships. His record is 136-37-4.

—University of Texas Sports News Service, January 26, 1967

■ ■ ■

CHAPTER 6
Development of the Wishbone

The Villa Capri was the nattiest hotel in Austin, Texas, before it was torn down some years ago. Its most famous room was Suite 2001. Clerks liked to say Elizabeth Taylor and Richard Burton spent their honeymoon in that room.

When truth prevailed, guests learned that while no celebrity vows had been consummated there, the once venerable, now peculiar football formation called the "wishbone" was named in Suite 2001 (where University of Texas coaches, reporters and even such celebrities at actors Dan Blocker and Fess Parker and country singers Waylon Jennings and Willie Nelson, all Longhorn groupies, often gathered after home games).

Three games into the 1968 season, a new-fangled offense with no name and three running backs had just won for the first time, 31-3 over Oklahoma State. Everyone was in a good mood in Suite 2001, recalled Houston Post columnist Mickey Herskowitz. Players, coaches, reporters had been asking all week what to call this *new formation when Herskowitz suggested it looked much "like a pulling bone," shortened to wishbone.*

"That's the way I had already described it in my story that night," Herskowitz said. "It was meant as a touch of color. But coaches liked to say it. So from that day on it was known as the wishbone."

Herskowitz said his only regret was not earning royalties on the name. Texas went on to win 30 consecutive games and a national championship in 1969, losing finally to Notre Dame in the 1971 Cotton Bowl. Texas coach Darrell Royal was the "most-in-demand" coach at clinics in the spring 1969. Alabama coach Bear Bryant, eager to learn the wishbone during the off-season, reportedly went to Royal's locked office at 6 a.m. to wait for Royal.

The wishbone did so much for the well-being of so many Texans, Emory Bellard might as well have invented the light bulb or the telephone.

"Well, it's not nearly as lucrative," said Bellard, an assistant coach at Texas from 1967 to 1971. "Every coach would like to make some contribution to a game they really care about. I'm no different. I guess it's a thing of pride."

—Hugo Kugiya, *Seattle Times*, October 28, 1994

It seems like when I started coaching in the 1940s and 1950s, the teams that won the passing title in the nation in most instances weren't undefeated or anything like that. It was teams with a powerful running back and that type of football, teams that used play-action passes with their running game, that were winning the national championship on the college level, like Bud Wilkinson's split-T offense at Oklahoma.

The last year I coached at Ingleside before I went to Breckenridge, I was moving to the concept of the wishbone. The quarterback at Ingleside could throw the ball because he had been working since I had been there to develop as a passer. He was also quick and could run and do some things.

The triple option of the wishbone can be seen as Texas quarterback Eddie Phillips prepares to hand off to fullback Steve Worster. Halfbacks Jim Bertelsen (35) and Terry Collins (33) complete the triple option possibilities for quarterback Phillips. (Photo courtesy of the University of Texas sports information)

I loved option football, so we started the first concepts of the wishbone at that time. We ran those concepts the next year in 1955 in the playoffs in my first year at Breckenridge. We were still lining up in the straight-T. It wasn't the alignment of the wishbone, but the concepts, although not exactly the same, were similar to the wishbone concept. I didn't know anybody who was running this particular triple option concept. Worlds and worlds of coaches would show me an offensive formation and ask what I would do with it. That is not what the wishbone is. What I wanted to do was to find the best way to position those eleven people to carry out this plan. That is how the wishbone came into being.

The wishbone is based on certain defensive principles. When you send a receiver deep into the outside zone, you send him straight down the football field. Somebody has to cover him because you can't just let him run down there. Somebody has to acknowledge that you could throw the football to him. That is a principle. Now, when he runs off that line of scrimmage, the ball is either going to be thrown deep to him or whoever is defending him will be a long way from the line of scrimmage. If Number 1 has to cover the deep third of the field, if there is a deep threat, then Number 2 in the defensive alignment has to be responsible for the pitch.

The third man from the outside in the defense in that scenario has to be the man who is responsible for the quarterback. How they defend the fullback is dictated by their alignment inside the Number 3 man. If those principles are all there, the next step is handling those principles and keeping those principles, which is what the wishbone is. Those principles determine the operation of the triple option play.

Developing the wishbone

We decided to put in the triple-option offense that summer in 1968 after my first season at Texas. Obviously, there was some anxiety when the kids came back that fall because they had never done it before.

I took the old straight T-formation and moved the fullback closer to the quarterback—right behind him. The halfbacks were moved a step deeper and closer together, lining up five yards behind the offensive guards instead of behind the tackles. The two halfbacks were just two yards apart.

There were some anxious moments in the early stages. The base play that the offense is built around is the triple option. We had the fullback up closer than where he was eventually positioned. After the second game, we moved him back a little bit because he was making a little too fast of a read for the quarterback to really handle it effectively.

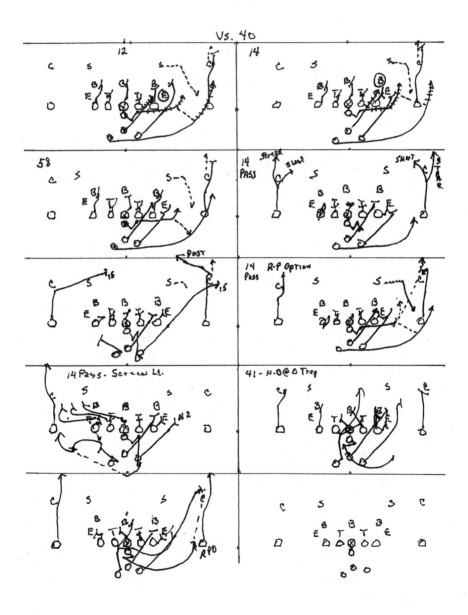

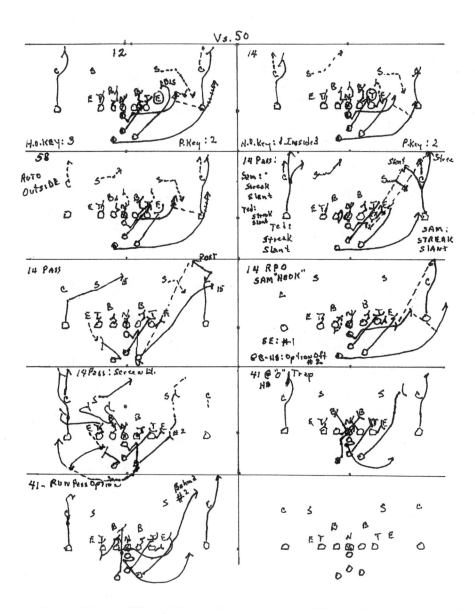

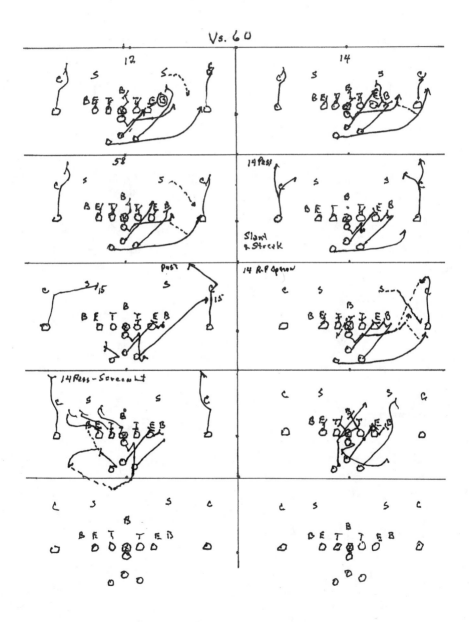

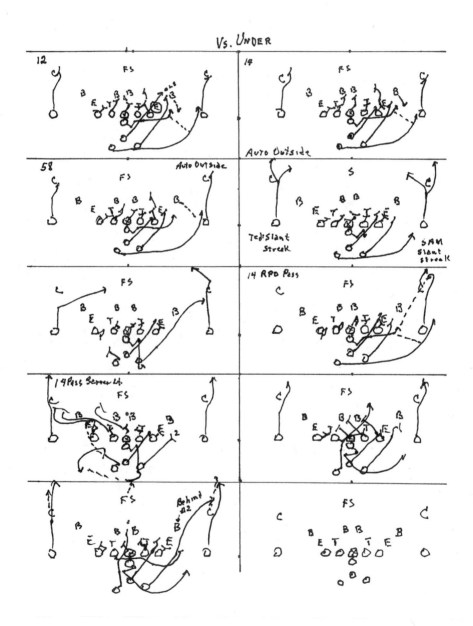

Darrell Royal had suggested that we might want to move him back a little bit. I think eventually we would have gotten it had we stayed with the pattern, but perhaps we progressed a little more rapidly than we would have if we had left him closer. So it worked out good.

Our quarterback was Bill Bradley, one of the greatest athletes I have ever worked with. He could run; he could punt with either leg—a great punter. He could throw the football right-handed or left-handed. Everything about him said he could be a great wishbone quarterback. He was the greatest player in the state in high school at Palestine. They called him "Super Bill" because he always made big plays.

The only thing was that Bill put lots of pressure on himself because he came to Texas with such expectations, and he never could quite relax there and use his team. He always felt that he had to make the plays himself. But as far as making the option, that sucker could run the ball.

James Street was just the opposite. He could handle his position, but he could use all the players who surrounded him, too. He was fiercely competitive, and he didn't have to go through some of the hard knocks and so forth that Bill had to go through with expectations being a lot higher. I never knew anybody who enjoyed playing football more than Bill Bradley.

He played quarterback, and we tied Houston in the season opener. The next week we lost to Texas Tech. We took Bradley out during that game, and Street played the rest of the time. We just weren't doing some things on the field. Bill's biggest problem was that he was running an offense that he had never run in his life, and he was at a starting point. He couldn't relax and use his football team to help him simultaneously. He took it great when we moved him from quarterback to cornerback. He played great out there. He was doing something out there that he could do and was capable of doing. He went on to play for the Philadelphia Eagles. It was a blessing for him. He would never have played quarterback in the pros.

■ ■ ■

I want to thank Emory Bellard for letting me be the first wishbone quarterback—for two games.

—Bill Bradley in his induction speech at the Texas Sports Hall of Fame, March 2009

■ ■ ■

I think the University of Texas football team became much better overall when Bill Bradley went to cornerback and gave us a tremendous player on defense, and James Street moved up to the starting quarterback spot. We improved that spot likewise, so I think that all the moves that were made prior to the Oklahoma State ballgame, which was the third game of the 1968 season, all ended up in the University of Texas' best interest. Our team started becoming a national power at that point. We never looked back. We won the rest of our games, and we got better and better and better doing what we were doing. We beat Oklahoma State in the third game, and then we beat the University of Oklahoma in Dallas the next game. From that point on, I think we got our team solidified.

Street stepped in and ran the offense. All he did was get better and better, and he was a fierce competitor. We tied Houston, lost to Texas Tech and then won our next thirty games.

■ ■ ■

"During the off-season, there was a lot of grumbling from UT people about three 6-4 seasons," Bill Bradley said, "and a lot of pressure was being put on Coach Royal. That's when he moved (Fred) Akers to the defense and brought in Emory Bellard as offensive coordinator, and he invented the Wishbone. I never liked it much myself, but, God, what an offense it was."

Bradley's experience with it was brief. The Longhorns tied Houston in the 1968 season opener and then suffered a loss at Tech—during which Bradley was pulled in favor of James Street. Forever.

"I did not run that offense worth a damn," he says. "Not near as well as it was fixing to be operated. It really started clicking once James started operating it. It was built for him, not for me."

—Whit Canning, *Where Have You Gone?*
James Street, Chris Gilbert, Roosevelt Leaks And Other Texas Greats

■ ■ ■

We won the Southwest Conference championship and beat Tennessee in the Cotton Bowl in that first season with the wishbone. Then, in 1969, we won the national championship. We beat Arkansas, 15-14, in that famous game in Fayetteville to win the Southwest Conference title, and then we beat Notre Dame when James Street drove the Longhorns for a touchdown on the final possession of the game to win the game 21-17.

We won the national championship again in 1970 with Eddie Phillips at quarterback. Donnie Wigginton also got to play quarterback because Eddie got turf toe. Notre Dame beat us in the Cotton Bowl, 24-11, the next year to end our thirty-game winning streak, but we earned a share of the national championship.

Teaching the wishbone

In the spring after that 1968 season, our coaches' offices were full with coaches from about every college in America. Maybe not every college, but it felt like it was. About a third of them were trying to find out how to defend against the wishbone. And two-thirds were there to try to put it in.

Darrell said Duffy Daugherty wanted to come down from Michigan State and talk to me about the wishbone. I told Darrell that Duffy couldn't run this offense. Michigan State had had a multiple offense, and there was no way with his philosophy or the way he felt about football that he would give his offense a half dozen or so plays and run it. They just couldn't do that, because it is a different technique. Anyway, he came down, and I spent some time with him. He went back and put it in along with everything else. That was just part of his offense. They still did things the same way they had always done it with the single wing and wing-T.

Why did the wishbone get so much attention after just one year? Well, it was different, it was new, and it was very, very explosive. I never have understood how people talk about the wishbone being three yards and a cloud of dust. A lot of people like to use that statement in describing the running game, but it was everything but that because we were rattling the chains and moving the football with a lot of success. We led the nation in rushing that season.

Pepper Rogers, the coach at UCLA, spent a week in Austin with me. He went back and installed the wishbone offense that year and won the Pac-10 championship that year. He had had a poor season the previous year. Mark Harmon, the movie actor who was former Heisman Trophy winner Tom Harmon's son, was UCLA's quarterback and a darn good one running the wishbone. Well, they won the Pac-10, and Pepper had a book out on the wishbone offense before Christmas. He took everything I showed him and then wrote a book on it. At least he did acknowledge in the book that he had talked to me.

Teaching Bear and the Tide

I don't know if the story about Bear Bryant waiting for Darrell at his office at 6 a.m. is true, but I do know that Darrell called and said he and I had been invited to speak at the Alabama high school coaches' convention in Tuscaloosa, Ala. In the process, he said, we were going to spend two or three days with Coach Bryant and his Alabama staff and give them the wishbone information because they wanted to implement the wishbone. He said Alabama was going to open the season with Southern Cal, and they wanted to open with the wish-bone against Southern Cal.

They picked us up from the plane, and they wined and dined us that night in Tuscaloosa. The next day we were introduced at the high school clinic there. I spoke first. When Darrell got up to talk, he asked the group if they wanted to hear him talk or would they rather bring me back up there to finish what I was talking about. They said to bring me back up. It was all in jest, but I did all the talking at the clinic.

Then I met for two-and-a-half days with the Alabama coaching staff in a motel room where we were staying. I gave them all the information on the wishbone, all the blocking principles and all the details of defenses that you could play against it. That was one reason the wishbone was so effective in the early years—people had to adapt their defensive fronts to defend against it. Our blocking schemes were set up to go against the "forty," "fifty," "sixty" or "under" defenses. These were defensive recognitions.

They were all predicated on the position of the Number 3 man and the people on his inside. Number 3 in the defensive structure has always got to be responsible for the quarterback. The Number 2 man has to defend the pitch, and Number 3 always has the quarterback. There are just basic defensive prin-ciples. If the first man inside the Number 3 man is the linebacker and the second man inside is down, that has to be a "forty" defense on recognition. If the first man inside the Number 3 man was down and the second man was up, that was a "fifty "defense. If both the first man and the second man were down inside the Number 3 man, that was "sixty." If the first two men inside of the Number 3 man were inside the offensive tackle, that was "under."

There wasn't a bunch of other things the defenses could do. All the block-ing principles were set up to whip those four situations. We would prepare all week on the defense that a team normally played, but then we would go into the game and they would be playing a wide-tackle-six or a split-six—something they had never played before—but we could adjust to a "sixty" or "under" blocking scheme really quick.

I'll tell you a funny story about our meeting with the Alabama staff. The halfbacks in the wishbone never take their first step straight ahead; it is always lateral or swaying and then going back into something. So it is imperative that they be in a very balanced position. If they use cross-over steps, they will always run a soft arch when they are turning to run one way or the other.

We were in the motel room with Coach Bryant and his staff, and I said that these halfbacks have to get their feet completely parallel and even with their hands. John David Crow (the former Heisman Trophy winner from Texas A&M) was on the Alabama staff, and he said, "I think a better stance is a staggered stance." I told John David that if you get in a staggered stance, I promise you your first step will be lateral and your second step will be a cross-over step and will bow backwards rather than staying lateral. In the wishbone, it was very important that the halfbacks never take a step forward. Their first step is always a lateral move.

He said that was nuts: "I have run that stance at A&M and I played that stance in the pros, and that is the only stance I've ever coached."

"I'll tell you what," I said. "I'll bet you. You get your film and you get your players that you coach and you bring it in here and you run it. I'll bet you that you run that arc."

Coach Bryant said to go get the film. They put the film on, and every one of those players in that stance took their first step forward, their second step to the side and then stepped back in that little arc or bow. They ran it time after time after time. John David saw what I was talking about, and Coach Bryant told him, "Change it." Because of that, Alabama had their halfbacks stand up with their feet balanced and their hands on their thighs. They wouldn't let them get down in their stance.

The first step in anything determines where you are going to go and the path you are going to take. The halfbacks always had a stutter step. It took lots of time to get that right. They used to take pictures of the wishbone, and they said they looked like ballet dancers with everybody in sync moving simultaneously together.

Longhorns helping Sooners

We scored on Steve Worster's seven-yard touchdown run on a late drive to beat Oklahoma 26-20 in 1968, the first year we put in the wishbone. We beat the Sooners again in 1969 (21-17) and 1970 (41-9). In the spring of 1970, however, after we had beaten Oklahoma two years in a row with the wishbone, Darrell said that Chuck Fairbanks, Oklahoma's head coach, was in bad trouble.

Darrell said: "I think Chuck is fixing to get fired. I want to help him out. Barry Switzer [Oklahoma's offensive coordinator] is going to call you. I want you to tell him how to run the wishbone."

I asked if I should just show them how we lined up. "No," Darrell said, "I want you to show them everything how we run the wishbone."

So I gave Oklahoma our entire wishbone offense. Oklahoma took that and added speed to it. They became the most prolific offense in the nation. We had plenty of speed, but we didn't have the kind of speed that they had. In fact, nobody had the kind of speed that they had at that time. Oklahoma's wishbone beat Texas five years in a row in 1971-75.

A year or so ago, Darrell called me. We were talking about giving our wishbone playbook to Oklahoma. He said, "I wouldn't be nearly as benevolent now as I was then."

Oklahoma's speed really changed the wishbone. It is just like everything in football—everything is relative. The better your guard is, the better your guard play is going to be. The better the tight end, the better the tight end play will be. The better the quarterback is, the better his play is going to be and the more successful. He is the engine or the director of the offense, so certainly his capabilities are going to be a big part of it. How much of a part depends on what his capabilities are. The better they are, the better they are going to do.

I think you can take four average players in the wishbone and come nearer to being successful than if you had those same four average players doing something else, because at least they would complement each other to make it tougher to defend. That doesn't mean they are going to be great. It just means they were going to come nearer to being successful.

That is why the service academies have had success running the wishbone. Kenny Hatfield started running the wishbone at the Air Force Academy, and he was followed by Fisher DeBerry. Air Force was the most successful military school during that era. The Naval Academy ran a form of the wishbone. They would line up with a wing on it, but it was the same thing. But the Naval Academy was successful during that tenure. West Point hasn't been successful in a long time, and it is the only one that hasn't run the wishbone.

Recruiting quarterbacks

Of course, the first wishbone quarterbacks, Bill Bradley and James Street, had already played two years at the University of Texas. James played quarterback in the wishbone his junior and senior year, and then we recruited Eddie Phillips and Donnie Wigginton. Donnie was the quarterback of that Spring Branch team that we played in the state championship game at Memorial Stadium in Austin when I was in San Angelo.

When I was looking for a wishbone quarterback, I needed somebody who could run, and you would like to have someone who could run and throw. You were looking for the optimum. And I wasn't looking for someone with a handicap of sorts.

You were looking at the optimum in both the player and playing quarterback. You find a lot of players who can do certain things, but a lot of times they don't have the ability to use the other parts of your team. I've always felt that was Bill Bradley's problem on the fast adjustments we had. He had always run out of the I-formation, and everything that he did was him rather than utilizing the other members of the team to do something. It wasn't because he was selfish or anything—it was just what he had done all his life.

In the wishbone, it is what you read that is what you ought to do against the defense. Eddie Phillips was an excellent, excellent quarterback, and Donnie Wigginton could run the heck out of it. He wasn't the athlete that Phillips was. He wasn't as big or as fast, but he could run the option and run the football team. He could play and win. James Street could do anything. He had great innate leadership. He was not a kid who requested to be a leader—he was just a leader. It was innate and natural for him.

We had practice fields across the creek behind the press box side of Memorial Stadium. We would cross the street behind the stadium and then cross over that little creek and go up on the practice fields. There were bluffs all around, and we were down in this little hole. It was hot down there.

That first year we put in the wishbone, I was working with the offense, and I would be teaching this or that, and about every five minutes or so you might have to move over to protect the grass. Darrell would come over and say, "You might want to move over; you are using the grass up here." Every time I'd get going good, he would make us move to protect the grass. There wasn't anybody as happy as I was when we got Astroturf in Memorial Stadium because I didn't have to worry about wearing the grass out. I would just get everything organized and have dummies laid out. When we got the Astroturf, we didn't have to move anymore.

CHAPTER 7

Rebuilding the Aggies

C OLLEGE STATION—*Some of the searches for the previous 22 football coaches Texas A&M has had have been lively affairs—but the latest low key quest ended Monday with the introduction of a seemingly low-keyed man, University of Texas offensive chief Emory Bellard, as the new overseer.*

Although he seems outwardly serene, the 44-year-old Bellard, who was given a five-year contract as athletic director and head football coach at a reported $30,000 per year salary, has been extremely volatile in the winning department. In 15 years of high school coaching—at Ingleside, Breckenridge and San Angelo—his teams won 139 games, lost only 34 and tied four while winning three state championships.

In succeeding Gene Stallings, who posted a 27-45-1 won-lost record in seven years at Aggieland, Bellard Monday emphasized the fact that he is basically a product of Texas high school coaching, although his role in helping develop the Wishbone T offense for coach Darrell Royal at Texas, after joining the UT staff in 1967, had earned college head coaching job consideration for him several times in recent years.

"I'm a product of the Texas high school coaches' system and all it represents," he declared at a Monday press conference after reaching agreement with A&M officials Sunday night, "and I'm hoping that what I do here will be a factor in convincing colleges they won't have to go outside that system in the future when they are choosing coaches."
—George Breazeale, *Austin American-Statesman,* December 1971

After coaching at Ingleside, Breckenridge and San Angelo, and then being an assistant coach at Texas, I thought I needed to be a head coach in college. There wasn't any money in it back then. It was tough monetarily. I think the offensive coordinator now at the University of Texas makes about a million dollars. I was making about $12,000, and I think I got raised from $12,000 to $14,000 in those five years. We won four Southwest Conference championships and two national championships, and I got a raise of $2,000 over the four-year period.

I'm not just talking about me; I'm talking about the other fellows, too. Of course, Darrell Royal's salary wasn't like it is today, either. Mack Brown is making more money at Texas now than there was in the entire Texas A&M athletic budget at that time—or maybe the whole Southwest Conference. The salary budgets for all the coaching positions wouldn't equal Mack Brown's salary today. It doesn't make any difference, but it was true of everything back then. It was relative. But it tells you what kind of salary changes there have been.

Greg Davis (the current offensive coordinator at Texas) was a student assistant at A&M when I was there. He was a nice young man. He is a good football coach, obviously, but he is making $800,000 or $900,000 or a million dollars. You can make it on that. I had reached a point where I needed to make more money.

When Texas A&M hired me, it was for $40,000. I got screwed on this, but it wasn't an intentional screwing by Texas A&M, and it wasn't an error on my

Emory Bellard (Photo provided by Emory Bellard)

part. It was a change in law—teacher retirement. You see, my salary was for $40,000, but they said if it was agreeable with me that they would release it as $30,000 and then I would get an additional $10,000 for my TV show. I agreed because it didn't make any difference at the time. All you could put into teacher retirement was based on $25,000. You were not able to put anything above that into teacher retirement because that was the law in all state schools and the public school system. Well, years and years later the legislature changed the law and said you could put money from things like TV shows in as part of your salary. So it was just a technical thing. Prior to that they wouldn't let anything that was listed as a TV show be put into teacher retirement. That cut back on my retirement pretty good. But it wasn't like there was anything wrong on my part or that they were trying to cheat me. It was just the doggone Texas legislature making changes and messing up a bunch of people's lives.

Getting started at A&M

When I was first hired by Texas A&M, I was over there virtually by myself. I had a secretary, but until I made some decisions on the staff, nobody was hired over there but me. I decided to keep John Paul Young and Dee Powell off the old staff. And Donnie Wigginton was going to join my staff. It was going to be his first coaching job, but he was still playing quarterback at the University of Texas against Penn State in the Cotton Bowl.

I didn't coach in the Cotton Bowl that year. Darrell and I talked, and he thought it was best that I just go on to A&M, and it probably was the best thing. We had already started the preparation. I think everything was pretty well in place, and he took it from there.

One of the most anxious moments I had was on January 2. We met for the first time as a staff. I hadn't met with them as a staff for one minute before then. I had a list of players, phone numbers and addresses. The staff came in, and we gave each of them a car key, a credit card, a list of names, addresses for

Emory Bellard with Texas A&M president Jack Williams, who hired Emory as the Aggies head football coach. (Photo provided by Emory Bellard)

those names, what schools they were at and so on. All the coaches were assigned to one school because of the list of prospects. The positions the boys played depended on which coach was coming to their school.

This is when I got the sickest feeling. We had completed all of that information that day, and the coaches were gone. What in the world were we going to do now? We didn't have one boy committed to come visit A&M. I was past president of the Texas High School Coaches Association, so I had a pretty close association with all the coaches in the state. I don't think any of them told their kids to go to A&M because of my association, but a bunch of them said you ought to at least visit. For that help, I will be eternally grateful.

Before that week was over, every one of those players on those lists had agreed to visit A&M. That was the Number 1 objective, and before the week was over, we had everybody coming and a schedule for their visit. I just didn't know if any of them would actually sign because we didn't have anyone committed. It turned out that we got the biggest percentage of them that year. Freshmen were going to be eligible to play on the varsity that fall for the first time, but we were going to have a freshmen schedule also. We won the Southwest Conference freshman schedule that year, and we also had thirteen of those freshmen playing on the varsity that year.

■ ■ ■

The senior class of 1975—the recruiting class of 1972—helped to transform Texas A&M's football reputation from mediocre to meaningful. That class moved the Aggies from the obscurity of the Southwest Conference cellar to respectability in the national rankings. And it certainly gave A&M a building block for a much brighter long-term future.

It's been 35 years since Emory Bellard—then the Aggies' first-year head coach—signed that memorable class that changed the complexion of A&M football. The Aggies have signed many recruiting classes since then that have been nationally recognized and highly ranked. But perhaps no single class in school history has ever had a more meaningful impact on the university—not just the football program—than the 1972 group.

In addition to what those players helped the Aggies accomplish on the field, the signing class of 1972 also helped A&M become a much more diverse university. That class marked the first time an A&M coach had actively pursued African-American athletes in large numbers.

"There was some racial unrest at that time, and we were the first real wave of minority students, especially in football, to come through A&M," said Pat Thomas, a member of the 1972 recruiting class and the first African-American player at A&M to earn All-American honors. "We had a group that stood out and stuck up for each other. There was no question that we were trendsetters. We had eight freshmen (who started in 1972) and five of them were black. So, it was an opportunity for us to prove that we would thrive at a place like A&M."

Bellard said he didn't specifically go after black athletes. He only instructed his coaching staff to solicit the best athletes. The end result was a 41-member signing class that immediately gave the Aggies a shot in the arm and eventually gave A&M a shot at the national championship.

Prior to Bellard's arrival in 1972, the Aggies had endured 13 losing seasons in a span of 14 years. A&M had gone to one bowl game (the 1968 Cotton Bowl) in the 14 years since Paul "Bear" Bryant had left College Station for Alabama in 1957. And the three coaches who succeeded Bryant at A&M (Jim Myers, Hank Foldberg and Gene Stallings) couldn't consistently succeed on the recruiting trail.

—Rusty Burson, *12th Man Magazine,* December 2007

■ ■ ■

That class was something special. Those young men helped to change things in a very positive way. We talked to our staff, and our staff understood that the only things we were basing our recruiting on were playing ability and character. All that other stuff went out the window.

One of the standouts in that first recruiting class was Ed Simonini, a linebacker. But he wasn't that heavily recruited coming out of high school. When I was in San Angelo, we had a press conference with the head coaches in the Little Southwest Conference each year in August, and one year we had it in Abilene. I distinctly remember sitting down and visiting with Mr. Simonini. Ed's older brother played wingback at Abilene High when Wally Bullington was coaching there.

John Paul Young on my staff was from Abilene and had played for Chuck Moser at Abilene High. He came into my office and said the Simonini family had moved to Las Vegas, and Ed was going to school out there. Anyway, we got films and looked at him. He was certainly undersized. He weighed about 180, and he was playing in Las Vegas, which wasn't known for its high school football. But I knew his brother was a pretty good football player. So we visited

Emory Bellard with Dr. Chuck Samson, head of the civil engineering school and president of the athletic council during Bellard's tenure as the head coach at Texas A&M. (Photo provided by Emory Bellard)

with him and lined him up for a visit, and he came out. He wasn't very big, but he was a strong-built small man with a big neck.

He came to A&M, and what a football player he was! A tough football player. He could really move and was fiercely competitive. He started as an outside linebacker that first year. He was four-time all-Southwest Conference. He went on to be an All-American and was drafted in the third round by the Baltimore Colts.

I remember talking to the Colts' coach the day before the NFL draft. He asked if Simonini was big enough. "I'll tell you what," I said. "If you don't want a guy that size playing linebacker for you on your football team, the best thing you can do is not draft him. Because I will promise you that if you draft him, he will be your starting linebacker. You can bet on that. But if you don't want one that size, don't ever take him. If you do, you're going to be playing with one that size because he will make your football team."

He did, too. He and our other outside linebacker, Garth Ten Naple, played as freshmen that first year. We had thirteen of those kids starting as freshmen. We also got a pair of middle linebackers—Robert Jackson and Joe Bob McCrumbly—out of junior college who played that year.

That first class had everything except a quarterback. We started out with the quarterback who was there. I thought we were going to get a kid out of Hurst L. D. Bell who had run the wishbone in high school, but he went to Oklahoma. So we missed on him and signed a boy from Pampa. He was a good football player, but he wasn't probably exactly what you needed in college. But he was a good kid and led the freshmen team, and we won the Southwest Conference freshman title that year.

The next year, we signed four quarterbacks, including David Walker from Louisiana, David Shipman from Odessa Permian, and Mike Jay, who was out of the service. Mike quarterbacked the team in 1975, and David Shipman quarterbacked the team after Mike got hurt in the Texas game. Walker was our quarterback in 1976.

We recruited two wishbone quarterbacks in '76: Mike Mosley from Humble and David Bealle out of Arkansas. Mosley's dad was a coach at Humble, and Bealle is now on my son's staff at Bryan. They were both good quarterbacks, but Mike could fly. He was just what you were looking for. He could score from way out and do a bunch of things. He was our quarterback in 1977.

A costly decision

In 1975, the Aggies appeared to be the best team in the country. After A&M beat Texas 20-10 on the day after Thanksgiving, Bellard's Aggies were 10-0, ranked No. 2 in the country behind Ohio State and had the No. 1 defense in the land.

All that remained between a perfect regular season and a possible shot at the national championship was a Dec. 6 game against an 8-2 Arkansas team. Originally, the game had been scheduled to be played on Nov. 1, but it was moved to after the Texas game to accommodate ABC-TV's national broadcast.

That decision to move the game—agreed upon for monetary purposes by A&M and Arkansas officials—turned out to be one of the most controversial and haunting moves in Texas A&M history. Eight days after beating Texas, the Aggies were missing their starting quarterback, and, more important, had no emotion left. Consequently, A&M lost to the physically inferior but emotionally charged Razorbacks, 31-6.

Instead of a shot at the national title on New Year's Day (No. 1 Ohio State lost in the Rose Bowl, setting the stage for A&M), the Aggies settled for a three-way tie for the Southwest Conference championship and a Liberty Bowl appearance against Southern California. Drained and discouraged, A&M had absolutely no interest in the Liberty Bowl and lost 20-0.

—Rusty Burson, *12th Man Magazine*, October 5, 1996

■ ■ ■

At the start of the 1975 season, the TV people wanted to move the Arkansas-A&M game from the normal spot in the front half of the schedule to the week after the Texas game and play it on national television. We agreed to do it for the money and all that.

It was a bad mistake because we played Texas and won. Texas had already beaten Arkansas in the regular season. Plus, we lost Mike Jay, our quarterback. He got his jaw broken in the Texas game at College Station and couldn't play. We didn't perform very well against Arkansas.

That was probably the hardest college loss I ever had. So the Southwest Conference finished in a three-way tie among A&M, Texas and Arkansas. Arkansas got to represent the Southwest Conference in the Cotton Bowl because it was the team that was the last one to have been to the Cotton Bowl.

Gene Stallings and A&M had beaten Texas my first year at Texas in 1967 and got to go to the Cotton Bowl. Texas then had a six-year run on the Southwest Conference championship in 1968-73, so Arkansas got to go to the Cotton Bowl. It wasn't anything tied to the scores of the games or anything like what happened in the Big 12 South in 2008.

Incidentally, that game in the Liberty Bowl was John McKay's last game as coach at Southern Cal.

A time of change

In an era that would hold so many changes for A&M, the hiring of Emory Bellard was the first. He was a prime assistant on Darrell Royal's Texas staff and the developer of the celebrated Wishbone offense that was key to UT's national championships in 1969 and '70.

Bellard clearly possessed a brilliant football mind. His five years on Royal's staff comprised his entire college coaching experience, but he was a famous Texas high school coaching figure who took an assistant's job under Royal to better position himself for a major college head coaching job.

When A&M decided to fire Gene Stallings with one year left on his contract, Aggie officials soon decided Bellard was the right choice to build a new program. He had climbed the ladder of Texas high school coaching impressively, with a 139-34-3 record in 15 years at Ingleside, Breckenridge and San Angelo that included two state championships and a share of a third. As past president of the Texas High School Coaches Association, Bellard boasted a thorough knowledge of the coaches and schools in the state where the Aggies must sign a lot of blue-chip recruits to succeed.

Bellard and his staff, full of coaches with strong Texas high school roots including a young R.C. Slocum, signed two of the best recruiting classes in A&M and Southwest Conference history in 1972 and '73. These were the first two years since 1947 that freshmen were eligible to play varsity football in the SWC, and this enabled Bellard's young talent to mature sooner. Over the next four seasons, 1974-77, A&M averaged nine wins a year and was a consistent title contender.

"We had a good commodity to sell," Bellard said. "We had to convince the top kids they could build their own winning tradition at A&M. We sold the future of football at A&M, and the value of a degree from a respected university. And parents liked the conservative nature of the school.

"It was an exciting time around A&M. The school had gone through a great transition, from an all-male student body to 50 percent female enrollment. The Bryan-College Station area had gone from a small community to one of the fastest-growing areas in the nation."

Aggie rosters were filled with big-play guys in those years. Athletes like Bubba Bean, Pat Thomas, Richard Osborne, Carl Roaches, George Woodard, Tim Gray, Tony Franklin, Ed Simonini, Lester "The Molester" Hayes, Edgar Fields and Curtis Dickey would move on to strong NFL careers. And as the won-lost record improved, so did alumni financial support and attendance at Kyle Field.

—Sam Blair, *Aggies Handbook: Stories Stats and Stuff About Texas A&M Football*

When I came to Texas A&M, the school was really growing, especially on the female side of campus. Texas A&M had been a man's school for a really long time, and lots of old hands didn't want girls there and didn't like the idea of girls being students there and thought only men should be in the Corps. When I went there, it was about 12,000 students, I guess, and there only about 2,500 still in the Corps.

Of course, that really irked some of those old fellows around there and across the country. They thought everybody should be in the Corps and there shouldn't be any girls there. But we were becoming the most popular school in the country as far as applications from the young ladies. The girls had a great desire to go to Texas A&M, and it was really growing from that respect.

Don't misunderstand me. The leaders of the Corps were the leaders on campus. I had to meet with the leaders of the Corps on several different occasions and explain to them that we were in a changing situation. I told them that no one coming in to that campus wanted to deviate or stray from the traditions that Texas A&M had been built around, but if they didn't watch themselves, they were going to restrict them. They didn't care if the other students came to yell practice or pep rallies or anything, but they shunned the other students a little bit instead of saying, "Come on."

That is all those students wanted, but the Corps and a lot of the old hands didn't want them to be a part of it because they didn't fit the criteria that they had set up years ago. Anyhow, I spent a lot of time with the leadership of the Corps. I told them that those students not in the Corps already outnumbered them four to one on campus, and there was going to come a time when they were going to put their foot down and do what they wanted to do. I said that right now they wanted to be a part of the traditions that have been passed down. I told the Corps leadership, "There is going to come a time when they want to say, 'Let's vote on it,' and they will vote you down every time because they outnumber you." Finally, they said, "Come on and join us," and the students went right over and joined them. It was fine from that point on, but it was touch-and-go there for a while. They were fixing to bring about changes because they didn't want to be excluded from being Aggies. The good boys in the Corps said, "We'll let you in as Aggies," and then everything was solid.

Title IX, which provided equal opportunity in sports for women, also came along while I was athletic director at Texas A&M. Universities were faced with the additional financial burden of adding women's athletics. We worked hard to get our women's program to where it needed to be. We had some great lady coaches who were working hard to get a women's athletic program started at Texas A&M.

One of the challenges came when the women's groups wanted equal money spent on the women's program compared to the total men's athletic program, including football. For example, if the men's basketball team had fifteen scholarships, they wanted twenty-five for the women's basketball team. I had a lot of meetings with them. I told them they needed to get some sanity and not ask for everything. I said they just needed to ask for what they had to have to start a competitive program. It worked out very well. When I was inducted into the Texas A&M Athletic Hall of Fame, many of the former female athletes came to thank me for what I did in helping get the women's sports program started at A&M.

The Walkover

The Aggies love all their traditions, and the "Walkover" is one of those traditions that started when I was there. But it wasn't anything specifically designed or anything we planned. It just turned out that way.

I helped build the new athletic dorm at Texas A&M. It was a beautiful facility. I think we moved into it my third year at A&M. The old dorm was about two or three blocks farther than the new dorm from the stadium, so we always went on the bus over to the stadium. The first year we had the new dorm, I said there was no sense in us getting on the bus out there because we would be at the stadium within a block. So I said we would just walk over.

When we did that the first time, there were a lot of people milling around in front of the stadium like there always are. They saw us, and then there were questions asked. "Are you going to do that all the time?" Well, the first thing you know, it got out that we were walking over, and it became known as the "Walkover." But it wasn't by any kind of promotion. It just kind of happened.

After that, when we started down the street that we walked on, it was solid on both sides of the street with people cheering and hollering and all that. The

The Texas A&M team walks from the athletic dormitory to Kyle Field before the game. This "walk" became an Aggie tradition, while Emory Bellard was the head coach at A&M. (Photo provided by Emory Bellard)

band was at the other end playing the *Aggie War Hymn* as we went into the stadium. We went under the stands right there and into the dressing rooms.

When we got to A&M, they had all those great traditions like the Twelfth Man, but they were traditions of people. All those traditions are outstanding and tell a story, but they don't win football games. After Bear Bryant left, they had had only one or two successful seasons until we got there. The reason for the traditions wasn't the standard-bearer of football.

The first thing we did to turn around the football program at A&M was recruitment. At Texas A&M, I didn't have to worry about if I was going to have the support of the president or whether we could adequately fund the program that we wanted to carry out. That wasn't the issue.

They were in debt in the years before I came there. We came out of the debt while I was there. Instead of averaging well below the capacity for attendance in the stadium, we filled over the capacity of the stadium in attendance. Instead of the Aggie Club setting $50,000 aside for the athletic program at A&M, we set aside $500,000 for the program. We were adding stands for the growth of our program, and the student body was growing proportionately and simultaneously to the program. There were a lot of things coming to the forefront, and all of these things we had going helped with the "tradition" to win at Texas A&M. And we did win. We had back-to-back 10-2 seasons in 1975 and '76, and we were 48-27 in our years at Texas A&M.

Expanding Kyle Field

People like to give football a bad name because people are spending more money on football than they need to spend and doing things they don't need to do. But most of it is being taken care of by grants and that kind of thing. You can't spend tax dollars on those things, but a lot of people don't know that. They see money being spent, and they don't know why the library can't get that money. It is because the library didn't get that kind of donation. The state can pay for a lot of that stuff, but it can't pay for athletes, but sometimes that is not what that money is to be spent for.

For example, building structures that are part of the campus is applicable, and you can get state funds for things like that. We got state funds to help with our expansion of Kyle Field, but in the process we built physical education facilities for the girls on campus because there were no PE facilities for girls. So it was not just an expansion of the stadium. It served two purposes. Part of it was state-funded, and part of it wasn't.

We made a big transition, and we made it in a pretty short span of time. We couldn't build dormitories on that campus fast enough to take care of the growing student body. The school was growing, and ticket sales for our

*The Texas A&M band performs in the first game at Kyle Field after the
expansion that Emory Bellard helped design.
(Photo provided by Emory Bellard)*

football games shot up, too. Some of that was due to the expanding numbers of the student body, and a lot of it was just making more available
seats.

Texas A&M was averaging 26,000 per game at Kyle Field when I got there.
The capacity of the stadium was 48,000, and we went to an average of 5,000
over capacity. We put folding chairs on the track because of the demand. We
had been filling those stands, and we said, "You're not going to like these seats,"
but we were selling out.

The first stadium expansion involved reducing the size of the seats. They
had really had unusually wide seats for a stadium seat. It was really extra roomy,
and we reduced it. I went all over the country explaining that expansion jok-

The 1972 coaching staff at Texas A&M. (Photo provided by Emory Bellard)

ingly. I said if you had trouble before, you were still going to have trouble fitting into them. But I said we were going to reduce the size of the seats on that double side over there, and everybody bought into it without any problem. I think we reduced each seat by two or three inches, and it gave us something like 2,000 more seats.

Then when we started the stadium expansion, we added the third decks on both sides of the stadium. That was when we put in the PE department facilities and incorporated that into the structure that was going to be on that one side.

To have the funding to do that, we had to sell so many private boxes. We put those private boxes up on the press box level. Everybody said we couldn't do it because we had to have that upfront money and it had to be created by the presale of those boxes. We needed the money in the bank, and we sold

The 1973 Texas A&M football team. (Photo provided by Emory Bellard)

them in one day. We started that morning by going from the top of the list down to the bottom of the list of people in the Aggie Club. We sold them in one day, and we added the third deck and those private boxes to the stadium.

Good food is important

When we opened the new athletic dorm, we hired the sweetest, finest, most capable lady to run the dining room.

A dining room makes everything come together in a program because the athletes are eating there. If the food is not good or inviting, the other stuff doesn't work. When I was at Texas, Darrell Royal came into my office one day right after I was there and said: "Have you ever had any experience in the cafeterias? I'm talking about planning food and stuff."

I told him I had no experience with that, but he said he wanted me to take a whirl at it. The lady who was running our dining room at the University of Texas was the sweetest lady and the food was great, but it was the same thing every day and every meal. It was so repetitious, with no variety. We went

The 1974 Texas A&M football team. (Photo provided by Emory Bellard)

through a complete change in that regard and re-set the menus. Finally we moved into a new dorm facility right across the street, and we got a café there in Austin that took over the food service. They cooked great steaks. That was a Godsend, because they planned the meals and turned out good meals. Everything was delicious. So we restructured that and moved it into the new facility. It was in operation when I left the University of Texas.

When I got to Texas A&M, we hired Mrs. Davidson. She and her husband were missionaries and had been overseas for years. When their kids started getting up toward high school age, they wanted to get back into the United States to give them a chance to go to high school the last three years in the U.S. As luck would have it, she applied for the job. We checked her out because she had never done anything like that before. But the quality of the person was so easily seen. She took that over, and we had the most fabulous food and dining facility you've ever seen. Of course, it was a state-of-the art kitchen we put in the new athletic dorm with storage and freezer storage.

No one could come close to what she did at A&M. For example, she might have Italian food one evening and have red-checked tablecloths on the table

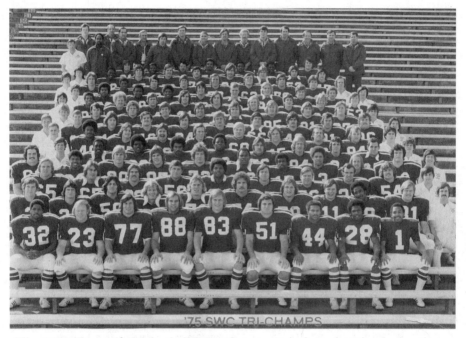

The 1975 Texas A&M football team that was tri-champions in the Southwest Conference. (Photo provided by Emory Bellard)

that evening. She had everything that went with an Italian meal and made it wonderful.

We had all our pregame meals in a special room, and she would have the young ladies there to serve. They wore evening dresses. It was such a tremendous program, you can't imagine. It wasn't equaled anywhere that I know of. It was good, and it was because of her.

She gave it lots of variety. You would go through the line some nights, and she would have bananas and three kinds of ice cream and all the toppings. The kids were allowed to make their own banana splits. She did special things, and this went on all the time with every meal.

Oh, the kids and I loved her. If the players enjoyed their meals, we had a good chance that all the morale would stay good instead of having people

The 1977 Texas A&M football team. (Photo provided by Emory Bellard)

going in and bitching about the food all evening. That tears up your morale. She was a Godsend and a very special lady.

Sun Bowl humor

Of all the bowl games I have ever been to—and I've been to most of them at one time or another as either a head coach or assistant coach—the one I enjoyed the most was the Sun Bowl. Instead of trying to entertain you all the time, the people out there in El Paso would say, "We're having a good time; come join us." It was that kind of atmosphere.

We played the University of Florida in the Sun Bowl after the 1976 season, and they had a breakfast at the Convention Center with creamed gravy and sausage and eggs. They also had some horses that the players could get on and ride. They had both teams out there and had a country-western band playing. All the men in each traveling party attended this breakfast.

The 1977 coaching staff at Texas A&M. (Photo provided by Emory Bellard)

At one point, one of the Florida players was supposed to get up and make a talk, and then an A&M player was supposed to talk. The University of Florida player was a good lineman, a nice-looking young boy. He said, "I don't know if I can say what I had planned, but I heard an Aggie joke the other day. I don't know if I should tell it or not."

Well, all of his teammates started yelling to go ahead and tell it, and then all of our team said, "Yeah, go ahead and tell your story." So he said, "The reason that Texas A&M doesn't have a homecoming queen is because they are afraid she would eat all the grass off the field."

Of course, it went on like that, and all the kids died laughing. A&M's speaker was our kicker, Tony Franklin. Tony is pretty outspoken, and I was sitting there thinking that when Tony got up to face those guys, whatever advantage we had we were fixing to lose. So Tony got up and said: "I don't know anything about

MISSISSIPPI STATE 17, ALABAMA 12

NOVEMBER 10, 2007 | DAVIS WADE STADIUM | STARKVILLE, MISS.

Emory Bellard was invited to toss the coin prior to the Mississippi State-Alabama game in 2007. Mississippi State was honoring Bellard and his 1980 Bulldog team that upset No. 1-ranked Alabama 6-3, a game that was voted as the greatest victory in Mississippi State football history. (Photo provided by Emory Bellard)

your homecoming queen, but I'll tell you one thing. You better have your shoe-laces tied up tight, because come Saturday we're going to whip your butt."

Everything got quiet. That was his only comment, and that was the last thing on the program.

That night they had a banquet where they gave out the watches and stuff to the players. Just prior to the Sun Bowl every year, they have this big parade in El Paso, and one of the participants was always Miss Texas, who rides on a float.

That night when we got to the banquet, they had all the people who were sitting at the head table in a special room for a reception. And there she was, meeting people as Miss Texas. Her name was Kim Tome, and she was an A&M student. Her daddy had been a good friend of mine, although I didn't even know he had a daughter. But later she came to my office and helped with recruiting from time to time.

She was a knockout, tan and blond. I told her what had transpired that morning about our homecoming queen. I told her I was going to call on her when I got up to speak, and I told her what I was going to tell them. She laughed and said, "Coach, I'll do whatever you want me to do."

So that night when I got up to speak at the banquet, I told about what the young man from Florida had said, and I asked Kim to come up and stand by me. I pointed to the kid who

Texas A&M coach Emory Bellard congratulates record-setting running back Curtis Dickey. (Photo courtesy of Texas A&M sports information)

Texas A&M coach Emory Bellard receives the trophy after his Aggies won the 1997 Sun Bowl in El Paso. (Photo courtesy of Texas A&M sports information)

had told the story and said, "Get a real good look at what our homecoming queen looks like." The Florida player stood up and said, "I'll tell you one thing, Coach—she can eat grass on my field any day."

It was good times. It was hilarious. We beat Florida, too—37-14.

We played Southern Cal again in the Bluebonnet Bowl the next year in 1977. George Woodard ran for 185 yards and Mike Mosley 184 yards that day. I think we had about 500 yards rushing as a team, but we couldn't stop them. Southern Cal beat us 47-28.

Resigning at A&M

I resigned in 1978, right before the Rice game. When I left A&M, our program was in the top 10 in the nation in wins and losses for the past three or four years.

In retrospect, I made a mistake. Dr. Jack Williams was president of Texas A&M when I was hired, and he was a great man. He was a great president and did a lot to bring that university to the forefront at a time when they needed leadership. But he had a severe heart attack the year before this all transpired, and he had stopped what he was doing and couldn't continue with his responsibilities as president.

They put Dr. Jarvis Miller from the county extension service in as president. I'm sure he was a good guy, but Dr. Williams had built up a great team. By the end of the year, every administrator in that school had left. I went in and talked to the president that week, and one thing led to another and I finally said: "The hell with it. I am resigning as of this moment." I wasn't fired; I resigned.

That was a mistake on my part. I shouldn't have done that, and I truly regret that I did that, but I had had it up to here with something, and I just reached that point. It certainly wasn't the best thing for me, because I put my heart and soul into that program at A&M. And we had a good program. We had gone from having 26,000 in attendance to averaging more than 5,000 above the capacity (48,000) of the stadium in just five years. So we brought the crowds of people back to the stadium at Texas A&M.

Stars of A&M's 1972 Recruiting Class

RB Earnest "Bubba" Bean: Two-time All-SWC, first-round 1976 draft pick by the Atlanta Falcons.

OL Glenn Bujnoch: Two-time All-SWC, second-round 1976 draft pick by the Cincinnati Bengals.

DL Edgar Fields: Two-time All-SWC, third-round 1977 draft pick by the Atlanta Falcons.

TE Richard Osborne: 1975 All-SWC, 1976 ninth-round draft pick by the Philadelphia Eagles.

WR Carl Roaches: 1976 14th-round draft pick by the Tampa Bay Buccaneers, 1981 Pro Bowl (Oilers).

DE Blake Schwarz: 1975 All-SWC.

LB Ed Simonini: Four-time All-SWC, 1975 All-American, 1976 third-round draft pick by the Baltimore Colts.

LB Garth Ten Naple: Two-time All-SWC, 1975 All-American, 1976 seventh-round draft pick by the Detroit Lions.

DB Pat Thomas: Two-time All-American, two-time All-SWC, second-round 1976 draft pick by the Los Angeles Rams, two Pro Bowls.

RB Alvin "Skip" Walker: 1973 All-SWC, 11th-round 1976 draft pick by the Houston Oilers, 1982 CFL Player of the Year.

OL Bruce Welch: 1975 All-SWC, 1976 ninth-round draft pick by the Tampa Bay Buccaneers.

DB Jackie Williams: 1975 All-SWC, seventh-round draft pick by the Kansas City Chiefs.

—*12th Man Magazine*, December 1, 2007

CHAPTER 8
Little Bob

B ob Spears owned a café in Aransas Pass. It was called "Little Bob's" and everyone called him Little Bob. I first got to know him when I was going to high school at Aransas Pass. I used to eat lunch there almost every day because we didn't have a school lunch program.

Ingleside is just a short distance from Aransas Pass, and when I got the job at Ingleside, he would give a big banquet for the kids at the end of the season every year. It wasn't for the public or anything. It was just for the players; they would go over to his restaurant and have a fabulous meal, all on him. He would tell the players that this was for no reason other than that they played great this season.

It was a really great gesture, and of course he and I had real close ties. We always had frozen shrimp in our freezer because he was always sending it to me. From the time I was at Breckenridge and then San Angelo, he would call every week, wanting to know if anyone was hurt. I knew he was betting on those games. He was from Breckenridge originally and was vitally interested in Breckenridge.

When I went to the University of Texas, we had a get-together with all the coaches. We went out to Lake Austin to ski and swim and cook some shrimp, oysters, catfish and stuff out there. I was the only one who skied; I ran all the way on the dad-gum beach on those skis coming in. It was cold, and I was about ready to freeze my rear end off.

Anyhow, a couple of coaches there did the cooking, and they had the tools to do it with. The next morning we were up in the office talking about how much they enjoyed the swimming and how much fun we had and so forth. Some of them said we should have gotten more shrimp rather than so much catfish.

"You all don't even know what shrimp is," I said. I was just bulling, but one thing led to another. Finally, they said: "Bellard, either you shut up or put up. We have heard about you and your shrimp from Little Bob's. It is about time you showed us something besides talk."

So I called Little Bob and told him the situation. "I need your help. You need to help me kill all these thoughts up here that I have been exaggerating." He laughed and asked if there was any place where I could get access to a kitchen somewhere out there on the lake. I said, "I don't know, but I'm sure there is somebody or an alumni there who has a cabin out there on the lake that they would let us use it for one night."

I had already told him to send me so many pounds of shrimp that we could cook up there ourselves. He said, "Here is what I am going to do. As soon you as you find a kitchen at a cabin on the lake, I am going to load the mobile home up, and my wife and I and my daughter and her husband will come up and do all the cooking and all the serving. Everything will be set. In addition to shrimp, we are going to have some fish filets, oysters, hors d'oeuvres and dessert."

"Little Bob, all I wanted was to get some shrimp," I said.

"I know, but it is all taken care of," he said. "When do you want us?"

I gave him a date prior to the 1969 season, and he came up with his wife and daughter and son-in-law, and they put on the dangedest feast you ever saw. They had broiled ling for hors d'oeuvres. The meat was white as snow, and, oh my gosh, that was enough to make the night, but then they brought out the shrimp and oysters and fries. And they had big ol' pies, this big around. They put whipped cream all over it. When the coaches went home, each of them probably took at least two meals' worth of frozen fried shrimp that Little Bob had cleaned, breaded and frozen. I took five meals home.

We went undefeated and won the Southwest Conference that season, and of course we were going to play Notre Dame in the Cotton Bowl for the national championship. Well, I get a call from Little Bob: "Emory, I know you are all down there on the campus by yourselves, aren't you?"

I said yes, all the students had gone home for Christmas and we would be reassembling at the Cotton Bowl in Dallas. Just the team and the coaches were in Austin.

"Well, I have been thinking," he said. "Would I have access to a kitchen up there, and a dining room?"

I said sure, and he said: "I'm going to come up there and feed the football team the way they should be fed for having to sacrifice being away from home for the holidays. I want all the coaches, their wives and families, and all the football team that is on campus to be there."

He came up and put the same kind of meal out for all those kids, coaches, wives and families again that he had done before. You can imagine how many shrimp those football players ate! He went in the kitchen and prepared everything himself. His wife, daughter and son-in-law helped him again. When the coaches went home that night, they had two or three meals of breaded frozen shrimp, and we had enough for five or six or ten meals, probably. It was just unreal what he did, feeding that entire University of Texas football team.

Well, he called me the next year and said, "Why don't we have it at a little bigger place this year? If you have it in a bigger place, I could bring enough for seventy instead of thirty people. I know you have some friends that you owe a favor to or someone you would like to invite and have something special for them."

So we had it out at Austin Country Club under the trees. We set up tables out there, and he cooked it there and prepared all that stuff like he did before. There were more than seventy people there that night. It was just amazing.

One of the first calls I got when I got the job at A&M was from Little Bob. He said, "As soon as you get your staff together, let me know and I'll be over there and cook them a good meal."

Just as quick as I got the staff together, I notified him, and he headed to College Station. We went out on a little lake there, and he prepared the same kind of meal again.

He was an amazing man.

CHAPTER 9

Moving On to Mississippi State

After I resigned at Texas A&M, I had several opportunities in the business world. Joe Courtney in College Station wanted me to go into real estate with him, so I was looking at developing some land. I also talked to West Point about taking the coaching job there. They asked for my suggestions about their program. It was hard for them to get the kind of players they needed because the cadets had that tour of duty in the Army waiting for them after they graduated.

I suggested that they tell their recruits that if the NFL drafted them, they would have that first year or first summer to try to make that NFL team. If they made it, the Army could then assign them to a liaison or public relations job. The Army spends millions on public relations anyway. The Army could let

Emory Bellard is carried off of the field after a big win as coach at Mississippi State. (Photo courtesy of Mississippi State sports information)

them serve in that kind of capacity while playing pro football. In other words, don't deny them that opportunity to play pro football, knowing full well that 99 percent of them aren't going to be able to play pro football. I thought it was a good hedge of the bet.

But the Army said there were traditions about the Corps and they are very strong in all their beliefs. There is nothing wrong with that, and I'm not criticizing them. I'm just talking about this one particular area. Later on, the Naval Academy started doing just that. Napoleon McCallum did that. He was serving in the Navy while he was playing pro football after graduation from the Naval Academy. I thought that was a good idea.

If you can't recruit, you can't compete. That is for sure. Our discussions about the job at West Point never got to the point where I said, "I'm not coming." The discussion reached the point where I think I could have had the job, but there were some reservations on my side, so it never got beyond that.

When I was at A&M, we played LSU every year when Carl Maddox was the athletic director there. I had known him for quite some time. He had retired, but he was going to go to Mississippi State and help get that program started as athletic director. He called and said he wanted me to go as head football coach. He sent a plane, so I went over to Starkville and visited. I decided why not, so I took the job at Mississippi State.

We had a tough season that first year, going 3-8. We started out pretty good. We beat Tennessee, and they were ranked in the top 20 in the nation.

This sounds like sour grapes, but it is not. Our left halfback went down with a knee injury. He was out in the open field running when he injured his knee and was out for the season. Our other halfback, who was a good halfback, did the same exact thing on a running cut and was lost for the season. Then our quarterback got his elbow displaced and was out for the year. We won the game 30-6 or something like that, but we didn't have any backfield anymore.

We took it on the chin pretty much the rest of the year. We moved split ends to halfbacks and stuff like that. We played hard, but they didn't know what they were doing. We came back the next year with the backbone of what could have been a pretty good team the year before. We also recruited two freshmen quarterbacks and had an overall good recruiting year.

The greatest game ever

You remember that I had spent several days in Tuscaloosa with Bear Bryant and his staff when I was at Texas to help him put in the wishbone. Alabama, which was the defending national champion and ranked number one in the nation, was still running the wishbone when we played them in Jackson that next year in 1980. We played all our home games in Jackson in those days.

■ ■ ■

What it might have been was Mississippi State's greatest football victory.

What it wasn't was a fluke.

Mississippi State 6, Alabama 3. Believe it. The Bulldogs beat the top-ranked Crimson Tide in the trenches, in the statistics, and most of all, on the scoreboard. The largest crowd ever to watch a sporting event in the state—50,891—can attest to all of it—that is, if they have left Memorial Stadium. They were in no hurry to do that Saturday.

Another who can vouch for it, like it or not, is Bear Bryant, the Alabama coaching legend who loses football games about as often as America elects presidents.

Minutes after his first loss since early 1978, Bryant entered the State dressing room and told the Bulldogs, "You did a real fine job. You deserved that victory."

Later, in describing State's win to newsmen, Bryant called it "decisive."

Decisive or not, the stunning upset ends Alabama winning streaks of 28 overall, 26 in the Southeastern Conference and 22 over Mississippi State. Before Saturday, Alabama had won 40 of its last 41 games and hadn't lost a football game since Sept. 23, 1978, when Southern Cal was a 24-14 victory. You had to go even further back—Oct. 2, 1976, for Bama's last conference loss, 21-0 to Georgia.

Sweat-drenched State coach Emory Bellard called the victory "as sweet as any I've been involved with," then added, "We played from the ground up, start to finish, and never once let up.

"This is a great bunch here who all decided they wanted to be something better than average. I'm proud for everybody who loves Mississippi State."

Better than average is one thing; better than Alabama is virtually unthinkable. But, for one splendid November afternoon, Mississippi State was. And, it's there in black and white. State had 17 first downs and 241 yards to 11 firsts and 180 for Alabama, which had been averaging 425 yards a game.

—Rick Cleveland, *The Clarion Ledger/Jackson Daily News*, November 2, 1980

■ ■ ■

Where would that rank among my biggest victories as a coach? Oh, that was big, but you know I've had a lot of really great moments that I have been a part of. I remember that Woodsboro game at Ingleside my first year as a head coach. We had some great wins at Texas, such as that famous win over Arkansas in 1969, four Southwest Conference titles in a row and the win over Notre Dame in the Cotton Bowl to win the national championship.

When I was at A&M, I beat Darrell Royal in his final two years there at Texas. We played LSU eleven times and beat them seven when I was at Texas A&M and Mississippi State. Coach Bryant had signed a ten-year contract when he was at

A&M that the Aggies played LSU every year in Baton Rouge for the money. I coached the final four years of that contract. We had some big wins over LSU.

But I don't know if I have been part of a game that was as emotional as that one against Alabama. After the game, the team had showered and left on the bus to make the drive back to Starkville. I had a car wait for me so I could stay around to do all the media interviews. When I finally got ready to leave after all those interviews, I walked outside and all those Mississippi State fans were still in the stands. It didn't look like anyone had left.

I laughed. You see, I hadn't been a part of all those losses during the last twenty-two years like they had experienced. We beat Alabama in my second year with a freshman quarterback named John Bond. He was a heck of player.

■ ■ ■

Several factors contributed to the upset.

Bellard was the one who originally taught Tide coaches the wishbone offense in 1971 when he was a coach at Texas. He worked with his defense all week and told his players, "I invented the offense. I know how to stop it."

That was obvious.

"There weren't many teams that know how to defense the wishbone, but they did," said Alabama's Major Ogilvie, who gained just 30 rushing yards on seven carries. "It's a hard offense to defend, but they had a great game plan. That was the only time I lost to an SEC team in the four years we played at Alabama."

Russ Wood, a star UA defensive end, remembered listening to Bryant's weekly radio show the next week. A State fan called up, with noise in the background, and wanted Bryant to know he was still partying.

"I'm glad you're having a good time," Wood recalled Bryant saying. "I just wish I'd hear from you more than once every 23 years."

—Ian R. Rapoport, *Birmingham News*, November 13, 2008

■ ■ ■

In 2007, that game was voted the greatest game in Mississippi State history. They flew a plane over here to Georgetown, picked up Susan and me and took us to the Alabama-Mississippi State game in Starkville. I got to be part of the opening coin toss, and Mississippi State beat Alabama again that night. That was right after Nick Saban, the new Alabama coach, had just signed that big contract.

Time to call it quits

We went 9-3 and 8-4 at Mississippi State in 1980 and 1981, which were two of the best years in school history. We went to bowl games each year. We lost to Nebraska in the Sun Bowl in 1980, and we beat Kansas in the Freedom Bowl in Birmingham in 1981. We gave them several of the biggest wins the school had had in years, including that win over Alabama.

But we went 5-6, 3-8, 4-7 and 5-6 my last four years at Mississippi State. My decision to retire was a mutual decision. There was a lot of dissatisfaction about the program. That is usually the case. We had some of their best years at Mississippi State, but I wasn't totally satisfied with it, either.

CHAPTER 10
One More Coaching Stop

When I resigned at Texas A&M in 1978, I felt like I had had it. I was tired. I know that sounds weak, but that is true. It was the same after the 1985 season when I left Mississippi State.

We moved to Kingwood, which is outside of Humble. We found a spot up there, and that was where we were going to be. I was through coaching. My wife's folks lived in Navasota, which was kind of in that area. We were sound financially. I invested in a plastic thing in Corpus Christi, and I spent some time messing with that.

Then one day I was contacted by a kid. He asked if several kids could come over and meet with me. I asked what about, and he said they just wanted to talk to me. "Sure, come on in," I said.

They sat down, and said, "Coach, we're not going to take but just a little bit of your time." The kid who played quarterback was the spokesman. He said, "We haven't ever won anything in Spring Westfield. Would you come coach us? We promise we'll bust our butt for you." All these other boys said, "Yep."

I told them I had been down all those roads, and I didn't need to be going down any roads like that at this stage in my life.

Then I was contacted by Leonard George, who was the athletic director for the Spring school district, which was about twenty miles from us. Leonard called and asked if I would consider getting back into coaching. I said I had done everything I could do in coaching; I was tired. He swears up and down he didn't have anything to do with those kids who came to see me, but I don't believe him.

Well, I got to thinking about it. My wife and I talked about it. I wasn't doing anything. I was sixty, so I was probably too young to really be retired. Then the school board, the principal and the superintendent called. Leonard had told them I wasn't interested, but they said to just come over and listen. When I got there, they asked if I would come and coach. My wife and I talked about it and laughed, and I said I would do it. I told them we would have a good time, and we did. It was fun.

A near miss

So I took the Spring Westfield job in 1988 after being out of coaching for two years. I spent five years there. We went to the playoffs every year except the first one, and we should have been in there the first year. I have never been involved in anything like that.

We had tied Humble, and we still had Huntsville to play. We lost to Huntsville, which had also beaten Humble. Two teams went to the playoffs then, so Huntsville was the number one team from our district. Who would be the other team in the playoffs came down to either Westfield or Humble. We had tied Humble and statistically we were way ahead of them, but the officials wrote down the penetrations (of the twenty-yard line, which was the first method to decide which team advanced in a tie game in those days) incorrect. I called the officials the morning after the game and told them that the penetration figures were not right. The Humble coach even said to me on the phone, "They are incorrect."

But the officials wouldn't change the report, and after the season ended the Humble coach said he would stand by the district committee decision. The University Interscholastic League said they couldn't change the official report, even though it clearly showed on the film that we were ahead in penetrations.

I had never seen anything like that. It was wild. Those kids didn't get to go on to the playoffs that year. That's what disappointed me. The next year, we won the district championship. It was Westfield's first district championship in football, and we made the playoffs the last four years I was at Westfield. But they should have been in that first year. We had more penetrations and legitimately were the second team in that district.

We played in the state quarterfinals three times, and, oddly enough, the last two years we tied the quarterfinal game but we were eliminated, one year on first downs and the other year by penetrations, just like that first year against Humble. We had three ties while I was at Westfield, and we lost all three.

But at least the school is no longer a doormat.

A great experience

My wife and I really enjoyed our time at Westfield. We moved to Spring from Kingwood because I never did like being very far from where I worked. We had good times together. The people at the school were great, and the kids were great. We had a good time up until I thought it was time to shut it down.

I left a really good team at Westfield. In fact, I was planning on my son Bob, who was an assistant coach at Katy, replacing me. I was planning to leave a real good football team at Westfield and have him take the coach's job so he would be set to go. But Leonard didn't hire him because Bob didn't have any head coaching experience at that time. I thought we had an agreement; at least that was what I wanted to see done.

■ ■ ■

The SWC spent its final days as it had much of the previous 80 years—locked in mortal combat between Aggies and Longhorns. There are few things on which Teasips and Farmers agree, but one is Emory Bellard. He was present at the creation of the wishbone at Texas, and he was in College Station four years later to rebuild an A&M program that except for one miracle season, had been in disrepair since Bear Bryant went home to Alabama.

I have a photograph of a young, lean Bellard showing the intricacies of the wishbone to Eddie Phillips and Donnie Wigginton, and the other of Bellard and Wigginton hugging Aggies on the sidelines after A&M beat the Longhorns five years later. And I recall Aggies and Longhorns rising to their feet a couple of years back when an older, grayer Bellard retired from coaching after a successful stint at Spring Westfield.

I recall the humor of R.C. Slocum and the wit of Darrell Royal from that night. But the thing I remember most clearly is the eloquent inability of Garth Ten Naple, a linebacker on that 1975 A&M team to express the affection he held for his coach. Ten Naple's silence, however, was as moving as anything Slocum or Royal could say, and the hug he received from Bellard was just as genuine.

"I'd like to think," Bellard said a few weeks ago, "that I have some friends out there. I know they have a friend in me."

—David Barron, *Houston Chronicle*, December 3, 1995

■ ■ ■

Life's tragic twist of fate

So I retired again, and we moved to Marble Falls. We had always planned to move to the Hill Country when we retired. We had looked at a lot of different places.

But thirty days later, Mary Kay, my wife of forty-four years, died of cancer. They had diagnosed her with cancer in Houston, and they had told us it was inoperable because of where it was in her liver. It had to be treated with chemotherapy.

The doctor told us we could have the chemo treatments in Austin just as well as Houston, so we went on and moved to Marble Falls, as was our plan. Then we checked in at the hospital in Austin to get the treatment she was supposed to get. When we were in there, the doctor said, "Do you know how sick she is?"

"Yeah, I know she's got cancer," I said.

"No, I'm not talking about that," he said. "Do you know how sick she is?"

I don't know if she didn't tell me what the doctors in Houston said, or if the doctor just didn't make it clear, or if he had told her separately. I knew she was very, very sick, but I thought it was treatable even though it was inoperable. But it wasn't. Thirty days later, she was gone. We didn't even get to finish unpacking.

CHAPTER 11

Organizing Practice

xpect More! Reliability-Durability-Great Looks. Built to last, Spectrum Scoreboards offer any color scoreboard, any mascot image, amber and red Spectralite LED digits, wireless radio and hardwire control systems, and animated and video message display systems. We also have the EB1 and EB2 timers.

—Advertisement for Spectrum Scoreboards in *Texas Coach* magazine

■ ■ ■

The clock that Spectrum made for me is in the Texas Sports Hall of Fame in Waco. When I first started coaching as an assistant, coaches would say they wanted to cut back on practice today, and they would say: "Well, what are you cutting out?" That meant we might not do this drill today because we did it yesterday. The first thing you know, they were cutting a lot of things out of the practice that I think are important with repetition on a daily basis.

So I came up with a time schedule that is predicated on a two-hour workout as a basis. Then, if you ever want to reduce the amount of time you are going to practice that day, all you do is change from five-minute segments to four-minute segments. That way it doesn't take anything out of your practice schedule. It just reduces the time you are going to spend on each element of it.

As you get more proficient at what you are doing, the less time it takes to go through it and take the repetitive efforts to keep it honed. So we had twenty-four five-minute segments. That is two hours of practice. If you want to cut back the amount of time you want to practice that day, you just reduced the amount of time for each segment from five to four minutes, and you have taken twenty-four minutes out of your practice time and you are working an hour and thirty-six minutes, and so forth. If you want to take any less time than that and not take anything out of practice, you reduce it to three minutes for each segment.

I came up with this plan when I was at Breckenridge. We had very few facilities at Breckenridge and very little area to practice on. All the backfield and passing work that you did with that group individually was done on the playing field. On the other side of the bleachers we had an area that was grass and had lines on it. It wasn't a full field in any direction, but it was an area that sufficed for line play. So the lineman worked on one side of the stands and the backs and ends and so forth, or when the ends were working with the backs, they worked on the playing field on the other side of the stands. So our timing element had to be something that was located in between them so we would have a coordinated practice to make sure we were getting everything covered and then made sure that everything was coming together when we wanted to come in for team play and unite the two groups.

We had a manager sitting up at the top of the bleachers, and he posted number one, number two, number three and number four on a sign through the twenty-four segments. He blew a whistle every five minutes, and that was that. Then we went to the next segment. He did that so that all the coaches were coordinated relative to the others. That way they would end up together getting done what we were supposed to get done during that day.

All the assistant coaches knew what the next segment was going to be. It was already printed and taught to our staff. It was already decided what we were going to do on that step and how we were going to teach the players. That is what practice is. You teach them how to do what they need to know in order for them to do what you want them to do. You've got to sell them on that. It is not whether you can *make* them do what you want them to do—it is getting them to *want* to do what you want them to do and what you are teaching them to do. When you get that done, you have the atmosphere and the ability to have it like you want to have it in order to develop your team.

So that is the prime reason why I started using the time segments in practice, plus we had to work at Breckenridge in areas where we couldn't see one another. During those periods of time, we had to be on the same page so we would end up the same way, not just on that day but at the end of the week. Everyone was together with all the individual stuff you were teaching them.

Electronics weren't the same back in my era. The clock I invented eliminated the whistle, the timer and all of that. Basically, it eliminated the boy sitting at the top of the bleachers, because you push in what you want and then it runs those segments off electronically with a big beep at the end of each segment, so you have a sophisticated timer.

I went to Spectrum and told them I wanted them to make me one of those. I said they could have the rights to it, but as long as I coached I wanted them to always keep me a timer furnished at no cost. So they did. They made the first one for me when I was at Spring Westfield.

They have been selling those for a bunch of years now all across the United States. I think they sell for about $2,400 to $3,500 a pop. They are called the EB1 and EB2 (or Emory Bellard 1 and Emory Bellard 2). They are advertised

in *Texas Coach* magazine and everywhere, and the Texas Sports Hall of Fame
has one. Spectrum put it together. I gave them the rights because I wanted
them to do something for me.

Repetition is critical

Of course, you've got to make decisions about what it is you want in those
three-minute segments, or four- or five-minute segments. You have to decide
what you want in there that you are trying to teach. And then you've got to
repeat it and repeat it.

For example, if you get in six extra points in three minutes with a full speed
rush. Well, if that afternoon you get in six more, that's twelve. If you start multiplying that by five over the five-day work period you have during the week,
that is 60 more plays. Then you start multiplying that by the next week, and
the first thing you know you've got about 500 or 1,000 times that you have
done that in actual conditions that you want to be in. You have built that up,
provided you stay with what you are doing.

You don't do things in practice to satisfy or have fun for the kids for enter-
tainment. You've got to do those things. At least that is the thing I believe in.

Kids come to know what to expect in practice. They become like a group of
trained dogs or pigs. They just fall into place. They know exactly where they
are going. That is one of the biggest things about time segments in practice,
because you are not teaching them how to practice—you are teaching them
how to play. If you start changing it every day, you tell them you're going to do
this over there and give him this kind of pitch and you're going to do that. By
the time you teach them how to do it, you've wasted all your time.

So what you want is repetition, where it just goes and flows. You don't want
to mess with them too many ways to do it. You take the one best way you think
there is to do it, and that's the way you do it. So often you get two opinions,
and at some point you've got to be the head coach and tell them, "This is the

way we're going to do it. We don't need two ways to do it—we need one way."
It takes too much time to do it twice each time doing it differently.

Repetition is what it is all about—to do it over and over until it is a natural reaction. That is what your practice should be—to train them to do that with all this other information over here that we have been talking about and all the blocking schemes. You've got to teach them how to carry out that plan on offense or defense or whatever you are teaching them.

I also think practice organization is important. When I went to the University of Texas, we put in the time system that I used at Breckenridge and San Angelo, and we put in the practice organization that used so much time on the segments on so forth. Of course, we didn't have the clock, but they've got the clock over there now.

They weren't doing it that way before I came. They had practice schedules, but there was no coordination. I'm not saying they weren't organized practices, because everybody has organization. But I think there are just some better ways to do certain things.

There were some coaches, or there used to be, who would go into meetings and sit around and "hem and haw" or play dominoes all the time. But you only have so much time, and it needs to be utilized. This was the best system I could come up with, and it was because we split areas to work on at Breckenridge.

CHAPTER 12

The Importance of Fullbacks

When people think of the wishbone, they think about the importance of the quarterback. Of course, he is really important. He is the one who makes it go. But I was probably as fullback-oriented as any coach in the country.

I have always felt like the fullback was in the best position, being directly right behind the center to hit every hole along the line of scrimmage because he has a better angle than any other back. When you have a man positioned right behind the football, he can attack equally to the right or the left. He is your base of operations because of his alignment. If you don't make the fullback the base of operations, you lose an awful lot. Some people don't run their fullback in their offense, using him only as a blocker. But I've always thought the starting point of a running offense is to run the fullback.

Offenses have a tendency to want to give a ball to a tailback six or seven yards back of the line of scrimmage. There is nothing wrong with that. But take Jorvorskie Lane, the big back who played for Texas A&M recently. They put him back seven yards, and it just gives people a chance to get in front of him when he's carrying the ball. I have always felt the fullback working four yards back seems to get in there so much quicker with more force that it puts it down to one guy making the play rather than three guys getting in on the play.

The fullback was always the key point of my coaching, period, even before I went to the wishbone. When I was at Ingleside, we ran the straight T-formation. Like all teams, every now and then we would break the "T" and do two right or half right or something of that nature to change the pace of things. Even at that time, most of the play series started with the fullback being the initial threat. The first year at Ingleside, we had a boy named Billy Fred Massey. His brother John played left halfback that first year I was there. Both of them were really good players. Billy Fred was a senior, and the next year, as soon as he graduated, I moved John to fullback. That is where I thought the emphasis needed to be. It was easier to get him better involved both ways at fullback rather than from a halfback position.

Bill Taylor was the fullback the first year I was at Breckenridge. Maurice Mehaffey played fullback after him, and then Dickie Rodgers was certainly an outstanding fullback for us on our state championship teams. He was a tough, tough, hard-nosed kid. He was quick and had great body balance. He was tough as nails and a real fine fullback.

Mike Tabor was the first fullback we had at San Angelo. Our second year at San Angelo, we had a good football team until he hurt his knee in the bi-district game in his senior year. We had to play Wichita Falls in the next game, and they went on and won the state championship. We would have played them pretty good had Mike been healthy because we went from about a 210-pound fullback to a tough little boy. He was a good football player, but he was a little football player.

He had to start, and then our starting quarterback Gary Mullins got hit in the head and got a concussion in the first series of downs, so Wayne Fox had to replace him. But Wayne had a broken right hand, so he couldn't throw with a cast on his hand. When you lose your two quarterbacks and then your big fullback, that is a big blow. We really got out of the game pretty fast because of the injury factor.

Terry Collins was our fullback on the state championship team in San Angelo in 1966. It seemed like everyone was playing an even-front defense then, which was an eight-man-front concept. That spring I experimented with line splits of about six inches. You could line our football team up in a living room on offense with the blocking schemes we used in conjunction with those tight line splits. The basic play was the fullback off-tackle play. Those line splits made that hole a little faster, and it also gave us the opportunity to use a blocking scheme that would be very, very difficult to execute if you didn't have people in a reduced alignment.

Anyhow, Terry was a great fullback, and I tried to impress on those kids that year that there would be points in the season when we would have to take the football eighty yards. I told them I wanted to be able to do that with one basic play, running it to the right or to the left with the fullback and being able to drive eighty yards without ever having to turn that football loose. And we wanted to able to do it against good football teams.

We worked hard that spring, using different concepts and blocking schemes. It all turned out darn good because it was good football when we did it. I remember we were leading Abilene Cooper 7-0 at halftime that year. We were going back on the field to start the second half, and Terry said: "Boy, Coach, this is great. I like it when it is tight like this."

"Get your butt out there, you crazy son-of-a-gun," I said. "We don't want it too tight."

We knew that at some point in that game, in order to win, we had to be able to drive that football eighty yards without turning it over, and they did that time after time after time, running the fullback off tackle from that base play. We had great size at the tackles, and we had good blocking tight ends. We called it wind-rowing, when those cleats would slide backwards as those two guys would come off together in the double team, each with their power step coming off their outside foot.

The starting point of the wishbone offense was the fullback. The defense has to honor the fullback threat. It seriously affects them when you are forcing them to nail down the inside. That means people are being isolated on the outside, and then you are back to principles that I have talked about, and those optimums—the optimum with a body on a body and a ball carrier running behind him. If you can get that, you are going to win the fight more times than not, and you should. And when you get the two-on-one option and properly execute it, you ought to gain an advantage. You also have the third optimum working all the time, which is sending somebody into the deep third and forcing somebody to have to cover him.

The first year that we ran the wishbone at Texas, we had Cotton Speyrer. He was an all-American receiver. When we first started, I made a mistake because I tried to include a short passing game. We threw the ball very effectively that first year against Oklahoma, but it was an isolated backside that we were throwing against them.

But you don't really need the short passing game when you are running the wishbone. What you really need is to make sure you are maintaining those numbers on the corners, and you do that with the threat of the deep pass. It was like the first half of the Cotton Bowl game against Tennessee that year. They had two all-Americans—an all-American linebacker and an all-American cornerback. They supposedly had a great defense at Tennessee. But Cotton beat that all-American cornerback twice for touchdowns in the first half.

It goes back to those principles. If you've got somebody going deep in the deep third, you've got to respect them. But it all starts with having to stop the fullback. You don't need to throw flat passes because of what you are going to create from the basic play of the triple option. You are going to create that situation where you've got a body on a body with a ball carrier running behind it, whether it be a quarterback, your fullback or a halfback. Those are the options, and you can't get better than that.

That first year we ran two wide outs, we ran two tight ends, and we ran a tight end and a split end. I played it all three ways as far as the ends were concerned. We broke the bone that first year more than any other time. Occasionally we would run two splits with two tight ends, and we would put the outside halfback into the slot, and then we still ran the triple option. Those were special situations, though, when we knew what kind of adjustments they were going to make. They would roll their defense around to meet this like most teams would do.

You lined up like this because you wanted them to make the adjustment where the man who was going to defend the deep zone back there was also the man in the structure who had to be responsible for the pitch. It is tough for him to defend if the tight end is running down the field, because you can't be responsible for the pitch, too. So we ran the base triple option then. Everything was normal, and every pocket assignment was the same when you're coming off the line and going to the deep third and blocking the deep third.

I remember we used that against UCLA when we played them in the Coliseum in Los Angeles. But we didn't run it much. The basic thing that we did was operate strictness on formation. Most of the time we had a tight end and split end, because we did the inside belly series that was the base call of our offense. We needed two tight ends to do that.

People always ask me who the best wishbone fullback was. Steve Worster, the first one, was perhaps the best. He was certainly among the best, but there were a bunch of them after that.

George Woodard at Texas A&M was a great, great fullback. Mickey Herskowitz, the sports writer with the *Houston Chronicle* who is credited with naming the wishbone, wrote an article about one of our games in 1976 or 1977. He said that there was only one Earl Campbell on the field today, and his name was George Woodard. I thought that was a catchy little statement, because Campbell was one of the greatest running backs who ever lived.

In fact, George was the leading returning ground gainer in America in college football going into his senior year. But he was playing slow-pitch softball at the end of July at College Station that summer and got a small fracture in his tibia, and he was gone. He missed that entire year; he tried to come back the following year, but I wasn't there anymore and he never came back.

He was good and big. We played Southern Cal in the Bluebonnet Bowl in 1977. They had a great team. That day, George weighed 265, and he had 185 yards rushing. George was a very nimble athlete. He looked like a block. He was that broad in every direction. He had real good hands, a soft touch so he could catch the ball easily, and he was light on his feet. But he was a monster in size. That summer before he came to A&M, he got in the Texas high school football all-star game at the last minute in Fort Worth because someone got hurt or sick and couldn't come. He was voted the outstanding player in that game.

CHAPTER 13
Oh, Those Kickers

When I first got there to Texas, Darrell Royal asked if I had ever coached kickers. "I've never not coached kickers," I said.

He wanted me to take over the place-kickers that spring, and I said all right. That first year I was at Texas, they weren't a good team. They had gone 6-4 and 6-4 the two previous seasons, and the one we had in 1967 was a poor old football team, too.

The first time we met at practice that spring, I let all our kickers kick to see who had the strong legs. We would start out about the twenty-yard line kicking field goals. Then we would move up to the ten-yard line, just kicking extra points. They were just flopping it over the crossbar for the extra points. "Is that all the kickers we've got on the University of Texas football team?" I asked Darrell.

"That is all the kickers we've got," he said.

"Well, we need to put that down on the list of things to do," I said, "because we don't have a kicker out there."

After some discussion, Darrell said: "I'll tell you what—we've got a lot of foreign students from Brazil and South America that are going to school here and are always playing soccer. How about I get a bunch of those guys over there and see if you might be able to find one of those guys in there that might be a kicker?"

That was when soccer-style kicking was just coming into football. I said that would be great, so that afternoon I met with this bunch of kids on the field. They couldn't understand me, and I couldn't understand them. But I put a ball down. I was trying to get across that you had to kick the ball over the crossbar and through the goal posts. They all nodded—yes, they knew what I was talking about. They would kick the ball off a tee, and it would come off that dad-gum kicking tee at about eighty miles an hour and six feet off the ground like a soccer ball. But they couldn't kick it over the goal post.

Finally, they got it over the goal post, but they would have to run seven or eight yards to do it. I said you've got to get up here and take a step-and-a-half and kick. Of course, they didn't understand what I was trying to say. After about an hour and a half of that, I went back and told Darrell, "Either you are going to have to find an interpreter or something because I can't communicate with that bunch of kids."

"You didn't find one?" he asked.

I said no, there wasn't anybody close. They were real nice kids, but they couldn't kick a football. They could kick it about six feet off the ground.

So I started working with Rob Layne, the son of former Texas and NFL quarterback Bobby Layne. Rob was effective from about the ten-yard line. We beat Oklahoma that year when they had the great running back Steve Owens. We won the game, and Rob was the kicking star of the game because he hit a field goal from about the twenty. I swear, I didn't know if he could make it from there. But he kicked that son-of-a-gun right through the heart.

Later I did have a good kicker at Texas. Happy Feller was the kicker on our national championship teams. He was a camper at Camp Longhorn when he was a youngster. I knew his mother and daddy. He was a good kicker.

Tony Franklin

Of course, I had one of the great kickers in college football when I was at Texas A&M. Tony Franklin kicked a sixty-four- and a sixty-five-yard field goal against Baylor in 1976, which was the NCAA record at the time. He also kicked a sixty-yard field goal against Florida in the Sun Bowl that year.

Back then, the rules were different. At that time, it was treated like a punt. If you didn't make it, it was a touchback, and they would bring the ball out to the twenty. So it was just dumb not to go for the field goal with Tony. When they changed the rule, they brought the ball to the line of scrimmage if you missed it, so that changed our philosophy totally concerning Tony.

I have coached kickers all my life and had some really good ones who had great kicks under all kinds of pressure situations. But Tony had the dangedest leg I have ever seen. Every day before practice I would get out early enough to work with him. But I had to almost kick him in the head to get him out there and work on extra points. He just wanted to kick off through the goal posts. That was his way to warm up.

Every day before practice, I would make him practice different situations on the field. I would give him one play from the minus forty to see if he could kick it seventy yards or kick it from midfield, depending on the wind. All the team would be there razzing him and hollering at him. He got just one shot. There wasn't a second one, although he always wanted a second chance. But, boy, he had a leg.

At that time there were three great kickers in the Southwest Conference, and they did a national story on Tony, Russell Erxleben of Texas and Steve Little of Arkansas. They somehow tested each of those kickers for the velocity of his leg in August before the 1977 season because there was a big to-do about it. No question, the velocity of Tony's leg was much faster than Little's or Erxleben's.

Tony kicked barefooted. Don't ask me what barefoot does for kicking, but he could kick the ball much farther with his bare foot than he could with a shoe. It was unbelievable. When he hit that ball, it sounded like an explosion. I would think his foot would be swollen up. There is no way I could kick a ball like that.

Dana Moore

We also had a great kicker when I was at Mississippi State. Dana Moore was from Baton Rouge. I remember one time we had LSU down so that all we had to do was kick the field goal and we win. I called him over and said, "All right, you go out there and make them hate you."

They were always riding him because he was from Baton Rouge and came to Mississippi State. He went out and knocked it in there.

He also had a kick against Ole Miss one night. We took the ball and drove it on the ground eighty or ninety yards against a hard wind. They had a one-point lead, and we put the ball down on the extra-point line, just like an extra point on the three-yard line. All we had to do was kick the field goal and walk off the field with a win.

Dana kicked the ball that night toward the goal post, and it started rising, rising and rising, and then it started coming back and coming back. It hit on the six-yard line, behind our line of scrimmage. I had never seen anything equal to that.

CHAPTER 14
Recruiting

I had never been involved in recruiting until I joined Coach Royal's staff at Texas. But recruiting is like everything else—it is time-consuming and hard work.

The first order of business in recruiting is the determination of who. The next order of recruiting is getting them, and of course the next order is taking what you've got and teaching them to play—to do what you want them to do. It is not looking for an opportunity to make kids do what you want to do; you are looking for an opportunity to create a situation to make them want to do what you want them to do. When that happens, you've got a good program going. They are committed when you get them to that point.

Sure, there were times I backed off from recruiting a kid because I thought he wouldn't fit in. The first thing is to determine who you want, and there are certain things that you say recruits must have. They can have this, and they've got to have that and so forth, and then there are always those exceptions where some recruits don't have all that stuff or only one or two of those qualities. But we always looked at it as though they had to have a certain number of those qualities and make the evaluation of whether you wanted him or not, based on all that. In most cases, the number one thing is: Can he play football? Lots of kids are good athletes but don't play football well.

We received a lot of publicity for our first recruiting class at Texas A&M when we started recruiting black athletes. But all I told my staff was that I wanted to get the best athletes who had character. Most of the schools had one or two black athletes by then, but the schools in the old Southwest Conference didn't really start recruiting black athletes until after we started that year in 1972. The University of Houston was already recruiting black athletes before we started, but Houston wasn't in the Southwest Conference in those days. They were getting some great players down there in Houston. Then Houston came into the SWC and won the first conference title they competed for. They had players who did a good job in everything they did down there.

Well, the recruiting started to go in our favor because Texas was still just recruiting white football players. They had been dominant in recruiting without any reservations. But after a couple of years of that, they started recruiting black players like Earl Campbell, and the black athletes performed well.

The recruiting process is so very, very important in college football. It all goes together. You can't separate recruiting from playing the game. You've got to recruit. That is the season you've got to win.

Recruiting Lester Hayes

Dee Powell was on our staff at Texas A&M, and he was recruiting parts of Houston and Galveston. I usually went somewhere to watch a prospect every Friday night. One day Dee came in and said he wanted me to come with him Friday to watch Houston Wheatley and Galveston Ball play. He said there were two guys on the Ball team who looked good, but he wanted me to look at them and see what I thought.

I said, "OK, I'll go." So we go to watch the game, but at halftime I told Dee to forget about those two players he was talking about because they couldn't play. But I told him to get the name of that defensive end who was running all over the dang field for Wheatley. We didn't even have his name as a recommended player. I told Dee to get some film on him and bring it back to campus so we could look at it. He could fly. He was just flying everywhere.

He was Lester Hayes. So Dee got the film; in every game we looked at, he was scurrying around the field. So I went to Wheatley High School and told the coach that I wanted to talk to the boy. So Lester came down to the field house, and the coach introduced him to me. I shook his hand and we went into this little room and closed the door. We were talking . . . or let me rephrase that: I was talking, and Lester was just sitting there. After about thirty minutes, Lester hadn't said one single, solitary word.

I had told him everything I knew to tell him, so I told Lester that I would be back to talk with him often. "I want you to think seriously about what you're going to be doing now, because I want you to play football at Texas A&M," I said.

He was still just looking at me. I said I was going to have to go, and he still hadn't opened his mouth. I shook his hand and looked him straight in the eye and said, "I'm going to get you to be a student-athlete at A&M. You be thinking about it seriously."

He left, and his coach came in and asked what Lester said. The coach was excited because one of his players was being recruited by a high-level university. "Coach," I said, "I don't think Lester liked me very much, because he didn't open his mouth."

The coach said, "Lester stutters, and when he gets to know you real good, he won't be so self-conscious and will talk to you more. He just won't hardly talk to strangers."

I visited with him five times and had dinner with him and the grandparents he lived with. His parents lived in Washington, D.C., and had some government job there. They were a good-looking couple. I loved his grandmother, and we got along real good. This went on and on with Lester, right up until the day before signing day. And he still hasn't said a word.

In the meantime, Lester had played for a state championship basketball team at Wheatley. He was one of six guys in the rotation on the state championship team, and they didn't do anything but play run-and-shoot. They won the 4A state championship in Austin on a Thursday night. That weekend, he came off the basketball court and went to a track meet where he ran a 9.5 in the 100 and a 21.6 in the 200. He could fly.

I went down to talk to him again the night before signing day. "Lester," I said, "there is not another living soul that is recruiting you. (And there wasn't.) I am offering you a scholarship at a great university and an opportunity to get an education and get it paid for. Now I'm getting tired of messing around. You are going to have to tell me if you are going to come or not come. I'm fixing to go try and find somebody else because I've got to have some football players."

He looked at me and said, "I-I-I-I-I'm coming."

Those were the first words he had ever spoken to me. He finally got it out. All that time I had been recruiting him at his house five times, he had never said a word.

Of course, he was a great player for us, an all-American safety. He was one of the great players in Texas A&M history. He was a great pro, too. He was a five-time Pro Bowler and played on two Super Bowl championship teams for the Oakland Raiders. He was also the NFL's defensive player of the year in 1980. He is not in the Pro Football Hall of Fame yet, but he will be sometime.

When he got to campus, I took him around and I took him to the speech department and got a therapist to work him. He could talk to me, but he had trouble talking to other people. He didn't have trouble around the other kids.

He stuttered now and then, but it wasn't a problem when he was talking to the players. And that got better. I wouldn't let any of the press talk to him until he got to the point that he could talk, because it was embarrassing for him.

I'll never forget him coming into my office from his speech class one day. He said, "Coach, I gave my speech today, and I didn't stutter one time."

I cried like a baby. He was so proud of himself. Tears were running down his cheeks and mine, too. Even when he went to the Raiders, I talked to them and they continued his therapy work. I haven't seen Lester in a while, but last time I saw him, he was talking good and felt really good about himself. There are not many times you find an athlete like that.

An unforgettable trip

After our first year at Mississippi State, we were recruiting two high school quarterbacks. One of them was John Bond from Valdosta, Georgia. He was the one who beat Alabama as a freshman. We were also recruiting a quarterback named Tim Parrington out of Baton Rouge. I was going to Valdosta the night before national signing day to see John and then fly to Baton Rouge to say "hi" to Tim because they were both going to sign with us the next morning. I just wanted to make sure everything went OK with the signing.

John's dad had gone to Mississippi State, so we had a connection there. I got through visiting with John and his dad, and we got on the plane to fly to Baton Rouge. We were right out of Birmingham, and the Birmingham landing strip at the airport was right straight in front of us. All of sudden this dad-gum airplane makes a terrible noise and drops about 150 feet. I don't know how many, but it dropped a bunch of feet.

I looked out the window, and the propeller wasn't turning. It was just sitting there. It was a dead prop. But we were in a perfect line for that airport. The pilot took that son-of-a-gun on in and put it on the ground. That was all my touring that night.

Tim still signed with us the next day. I didn't have any quarterbacks that first year at Mississippi State, but I got two good ones the next year. Both turned out real good. John Bond had played split end in high school and just a little quarterback. The University of Georgia was recruiting him, too, but they wanted him to play split receiver. But he signed with us and had some really good football games, like that win over Alabama. He had some great games against LSU, too. Tim Parrington was a backup to John for most of his career.

But I'll never forget the night before we signed both of them in 1980.

CHAPTER 15

Wishbone Success

The wishbone offense dominated the national championship picture through the late 1960s and the 1970s, starting with Texas winning two national championships in 1969 and 1970, Oklahoma winning two national championships in 1974 and 1975, and the University of Alabama winning three national championships in 1973, 1978 and 1979.

When I put it together, I wanted to make the triple option our basic play and line people up in the best possible position in order to carry out all the assignments that they had. That's where the alignment came from. The pitch man was in the position out there lined up behind the guard, and he had depth, too. Both were things that enhanced his ability to run wide in a hurry. It required perfect coordination in the alignment of the two backs so their blocking would be most effective. The position that they ended up in was the most ideal position you could put them in. Basically, you start with the concept you want to do and then align the players where they can do it best.

People always ask me today if I am bothered because not many people run it anymore, and they ask if the wishbone could still be successful in today's football. Football has always been a game of change and evolution. It is just what people believe in. The wishbone could be as successful as it ever was if you could recruit the players to do those things.

The pros have had such an impact on young players with all these million-dollar contracts that they are making. These kids coming into college want to perform, catch passes, throw the ball and play that type of football because they want a career in pro football.

The pros have such an ego. They did a job of saying that a lineman coming out of the wishbone can't be as good of a blocker in pass protection. That is a bunch of hogwash. Look at Jerry Sizemore and all those other kids we had at Texas who played good pro football. Cotton Speyrer was a receiver in the wishbone, and he made all-American and played four years in the NFL. The pros play great football, but most of it is individual talent. The wishbone is a team offense.

It is based on attacking the principles of defense. If you get as good a player as somebody else, you can win with that offense just as often as you can with any offense. I don't think anybody can argue about that because the wishbone is as solid and sound as it can be.

For a while after I retired, I had people coming to me, saying they wanted to put the wishbone in and asking if I would spend a couple of days with them. Everybody is running the spread offense now. But some teams will go back and line up in the wishbone.

Born to coach

I have enjoyed every place I have been, whether it was high school or college. First of all, I love coaching. I don't know if I was born to coach or not, but that was always what I wanted to do, and I had the good fortune to get to do what I wanted.

When I was first starting out, I didn't know where I was going to get a job. There was a crusty old athletic director in San Antonio. I went to see him for an interview because San Antonio had several openings. The first thing he asked me was, "What the heck makes you think you would be a good coach?"

Why would he ask me that? "That's what I want to do," I said.

"Lots of people want to do that," he said, "but what is it that makes you think you will be a good coach?"

I started getting sort of mad because I knew I was going to be a good coach. I never thought about having to tell somebody why I thought I would be a good coach, but I'll never forget that interview.

When I got my first job at Alice, I got a letter from Coach Emerson telling me that he was glad to have me on his coaching staff and talking about the commitment to coaching and the kids we were coaching and stuff like that. It was a good letter.

He put all the things that we needed to do and the children I was going to be working with in front of me. I remember reading and re-reading that letter. I still remember it. I was always proud of that letter.

The main thing was that I had a job. It was tight trying to find a job. I remember they posted job openings on the board at the teacher placement office at Southwest Texas State, and I would look at that board every day. I remember there was a posting at Spring Branch for a head football coach who would also coach track and be athletic director for $2,700 a year. Of course, Spring Branch is one of the richest school districts in the state now, but at that time it wasn't. It was just a little community before you got to Houston.

If I saw a job for $3,000, I thought that was for me. Everything, thank God, was so much cheaper then. I understand business and how prices go up based on demand, but I never did find out why you couldn't stabilize a price forevermore, like this is worth so much, and we are going to stabilize it so it will always be worth that.

People are getting paid $50 million to play football today. I am proud for them, but that is ridiculous. Like the wealth that Tiger Woods has. He is as good as any golfer there has ever been, but look at all the good he could do with the millions of dollars that he has. It seems like one generation is always behind. What was a real good salary when you started out is no longer good. If you have a good salary, it should be a good salary way down the road, but it is not.

My namesake, the banker I am named after, was going to have a trust fund for me to have his name. Then the bank went broke. My trust went away, but I've still got the name Emory Dilworth Bellard.

If you want to coach the wishbone

The offensive plays that are included elsewhere in this book and the discussion of the wishbone offense, of course, are not as detailed as a coach would want if he were installing the offense as a complete commitment. But if you are a coach and really are serious, I would be glad to spend some time with you in a more in-depth discussion.

I don't have anybody going down on a kickoff this fall, so I'm really not worried about any outcome; therefore, I'm going to the golf course and really get frustrated.

Good luck to every coach in America. You do good work, and America needs you.

Epilogue

Emory Bellard, who turned eighty-two on December 17, 2009, lives in Georgetown, Texas, with his wife Susan. Emory and Susan married in 1994, a year after Mary Kay, his wife of forty-four years, died of cancer. He is quick to point out that he has been blessed to have been married to two wonderful, supportive women in his life.

Coach Bellard can be found at least several days a week playing golf at Berry Creek Country Club, where he and Susan live. He has shot his age every year since he turned seventy-one. If you see Emory, you will also probably see Dulcita, his faithful canine companion, who can usually be found lying beside Emory's chair or taking her nightly walk with Emory along the golf course.

Emory said his oldest son, Emory Jr., a University of Texas graduate, had "a very unique career as a football player, not totally because of his ability but because he was in circumstances that yielded an awful lot of success."

Emory Jr. was the backup quarterback on the state championship team at San Angelo in 1966 as a sophomore. When the Bellards moved to Austin, he

Emory and Susan Bellard (Photo provided by Emory Bellard)

had to sit out a year because of the University Interscholastic League transfer rules at the time, but his Austin Reagan football team won the state championship that year. So he was involved with two championship teams, even though he didn't play in either game.

Then the next year, his senior season, Emory Jr. quarterbacked Reagan to another state championship. Reagan beat Odessa Permian in the title game—oddly enough, in San Angelo's Bobcat Stadium, where Emory Jr. began his career.

"His seventh-, eighth- and ninth-grade teams were all undefeated in San Angelo, and then he was part of three consecutive state championships in high school," Coach Bellard said. "You don't have many situations where someone goes all the way through high school winning a state championship every year."

Although Coach Bellard remains in excellent health, he has had his share of tragedy in the past decade. His mother, Louie Cass Bellard, who raised

Emory by herself after Emory's father died, passed away in 2001, a month short of her 106th birthday. Emory Jr. died in 2003, and his daughter, Debra Lyn Bellard-Young, died of cancer in April 2009.

His only remaining child, Bob, followed his father's footsteps and became a football coach. Although he didn't get the coaching job at Spring Westfield after his father retired, Bob has been a head coach at Sonora and San Angelo Central and is currently the head coach at his alma mater, Bryan High School.

Emory has six grandchildren and eight great-grandchildren.

Coach Bellard has received numerous honors and accolades, often heralding his contribution to football as the creator of the wishbone offense. But his coaching career, which spanned parts of six different decades, is so much more than just that. During twenty-one years as a high school head coach, his teams claimed fourteen district titles, five regional championships and three state championships.

At the University of Texas, the Longhorns took his wishbone offense to four Southwest Conference crowns and a pair of national championships during his five years as an assistant to Darrell Royal. He claimed a share of another SWC title as the head coach at Texas A&M. His Aggies and Mississippi State Bulldogs also played in five bowl games—both rare accomplishments until he arrived in College Station and Starkville. His Mississippi State team upset top-ranked and defending national champion Alabama in perhaps the greatest win in school history.

His career is remarkable, and his contributions to the sport of football are many, although perhaps somewhat underappreciated or even forgotten by some. Although the coaching profession is often one of trying to copy someone else's method for success, Bellard did things his own way.

"I know when I went to Coaches School," Bellard recalled, "people would say, 'Are you going to do it that way?' and I'd say, 'I don't know if I'm going to do it that way.' I listened to every word that anybody said at every coaching clinic, and I took notes. I really did, and I was always close to the front row, listening. But I never felt like I was in there to do everything that they were talking about. I always felt like I had my own ideas about things. That's not meant to be egotistical. Some people just believe in certain things, like the wishbone."

While many high school coaches look to college and NFL coaches for the latest offensive and defensive trends, Bellard took the organizational skills and an offense that he first developed in high school and brought it to the collegiate level, in the process revolutionizing offensive football for more than two decades.

"I have always said that coaching is coaching," Bellard added. "The pros have access to a lot of things. If a player can't cut it, they replace the player. In college, you have players that allow you to win. You recruit them or try to recruit them. If you don't, you are going to have a hard time being successful, so recruitment is very important. In high school, you take what you've got and you develop that. You develop a program that feeds what you are trying to do. Maybe the best coaching that is being done anywhere is being done in the high schools because you have to play with what you've got. You've got to adjust. You've got to be organized. You've got to stress the points that will help different kids get better. Work ethic will never be replaced by technique or anything else, but if you can take great work ethic and a very knowledgeable approach, you are usually going to find success."

Sitting on the table next to Emory's favorite chair in his Georgetown home these days is a tablet of graph paper. Yes, Coach Bellard is still drawing X's and O's, still trying to find more ways to take advantage of those three optimums of an offense that dominated high school and college football in the late 1960s as well as the 1970s and '80s, an offense that he claims will still work in today's football because it is fundamentally sound. Just call it Wishbone Wisdom.

—Al Pickett

Emory Bellard's Honors and Accolades

1960—Head coach, Texas High School All-Star Game, Dallas

1962—West Texas Coach of the Year, *San Angelo Standard Times*

1966—President, Texas High School Coaches Association

1975—AFC College Coach of the Year, *The Sporting News,* St. Louis, Mo.

1975—Academy of American Football Gold Cup, saluting "Emory Bellard of Texas A&M for inventing the potent Wishbone formation"

1976—Hall of Honor, Texas High School Coaches Association

1978—Distinguished Alumni Award, Southwest Texas State University

1992—Hall of Fame, Coastal Bend Coaches Association

1993—Distinguished Coach Award, the National Football Foundation and College Football Hall of Fame

1993—Hall of Honor, Greater Houston Football Coaches Association

1994—Athletic Hall of Fame, Texas A&M University

1995—Texas Sports Hall of Fame, Waco

1995—The Morris Frank Touchdowner Award, Houston Touchdown Club

1996—Lifetime Achievement in Coaching, All-American Football Foundation, Mobile, Alabama

1999—Athletic Director Lifetime Achievement Award, All-American Football Foundation, Dallas

2001—Emory Bellard Night, Alamodome, San Antonio, honored by *Texas Football* magazine

2004—Athletic Hall of Fame, Aransas Pass I.S.D

2007—Big Country Athletic Hall of Fame, Abilene

2010—To be inducted in the Bobcat Athletic Hall of Fame inaugural class, San Angelo

Emory Bellard's Record

Here is Emory Bellard's coaching record from 1949 through 1993.
Teams in italics indicate those on which he was an assistant:

Year	School	Record	Comment
1949	*Alice*	10-2	District champion
1950	*Alice*	3-7-1	District champion
1951	*Alice*	4-5-1	
1952	Ingleside	8-3	District champion
1953	Ingleside	12-0	Regional champion
1954	Ingleside	12-0	Regional champion
1955	Breckenridge	10-3	Regional champion
1956	Breckenridge	4-6	
1957	Breckenridge	7-3-1	District champion
1958	Breckenridge	13-1	State champion
1959	Breckenridge	11-1-2	State champion
1960	San Angelo	5-5	
1961	San Angelo	10-2	District champion
1962	San Angelo	8-4	District champion
1963	San Angelo	9-2-1	District champion
1964	San Angelo	5-4-1	
1965	San Angelo	9-1	
1966	San Angelo	13-1	State champion
1967	*Texas*	6-4	
1968	*Texas*	9-1-1	SWC co-champion
1969	*Texas*	11-0	National champion
1970	*Texas*	10-1	National champion
1971	*Texas*	8-3	SWC champion

Year	School	Record	Comment
1972	Texas A&M	3-8	
1973	Texas A&M	5-6	
1974	Texas A&M	8-3	
1975	Texas A&M	10-2	SWC tri-champion
1976	Texas A&M	10-2	Sun Bowl champion
1977	Texas A&M	8-4	Lost in Bluebonnet Bowl
1978	Texas A&M	4-2	Resigned at midseason
1979	Miss. St.	3-8	
1980	Miss. St.	9-3	Ranked 19th in nation
1981	Miss. St.	8-4	Ranked 17th in nation
1982	Miss. St.	5-6	
1983	Miss. St.	3-8	
1984	Miss. St.	4-7	
1985	Miss. St.	5-6	
1988	Westfield	5-4-1	
1989	Westfield	6-4-1	District champion
1990	Westfield	5-5	
1991	Westfield	8-3	District runner-up
1992	Westfield	10-2-1	Regional champion
1993	Westfield	7-5-1	Regional champion

About the Authors

Coach Emory Bellard spent a remarkable forty-three-year football coaching career at the high school and college level, where he helped teams win twelve district championships, five regional titles and three state championships in twenty-one seasons as a high school coach at Ingleside, Breckenridge, San Angelo and Spring Westfield in Texas. He also won five Southwest Conference crowns and two national titles during his collegiate career as an assistant coach at the University of Texas and head coach at Texas A&M and Mississippi State. It was during his stint at Texas in 1968 that he invented the wishbone, an offense that revolutionized college football and produced seven national championships between 1969 and 1979. He is retired and lives in Georgetown, Texas.

Al Pickett, a veteran Texas sportswriter and sportscaster, is the author of two other books: *Team of the Century,* which chronicles the seven years that Chuck Moser spent as the head football coach at Abilene High, and *The Greatest Texas Sports Stories You've Never Heard.*

He is the host of "Let's Talk Sports with Al Pickett," on ESPN 1560 Radio in Abilene, Texas, and is the play-by-play voice for Abilene High and Hardin-Simmons University athletics. He is also a regular contributor to *Dave Campbell's Texas Football* magazine and *Red Raider Sports* magazine. He was named the recipient of the Outstanding Media Service Award from the American Southwest Conference in 2004.

He is chairman of the Big Country Athletic Hall of Fame in Abilene and also serves on the selection committee for the Texas Sports Hall of Fame in Waco.

Index

A

Abilene Cooper High School (see Cooper High School)
Abilene High School: 46, 77, 148
Academy of American Football Gold Cup: 145
Aggie Club: 86, 89
Aggie War Hymn: 85
Aggies (Texas A&M University): xii, 75, 76, 77, 79, 80, 81, 82, 83, 84, 95, 107, 112, 143
Air Force Academy, U.S.: 68
Akers, Fred: 62
Alabama, University of: 137
Alamodome: 145
Alderson, Shorty: 27
Alford, Larry: x
Alice High School: xvii
All-American Football Foundation, Dallas, Texas: 145
All-American Football Foundation, Mobile, Alabama: 145
Amarillo, Texas: 47
Amarillo High School: 31
Amarillo Tascosa High School (see Tascosa High School)
American Southwest Conference: 148
Andrews High School: 32
Anglers Court: 11
Aransas Pass, Texas: 2, 10, 13, 14, 19, 99
Aransas Pass I.S.D.: 145
Arkansas: 79
Arkansas, University of: x, xi, xii, 63, 80, 81, 106, 129
Armstrong, Henry: xvii, 22
Army, U.S.: 103, 104
Atlas, Charles: 28
Austin, Texas: ix, xvi, xvii, xx 21, 47, 48, 50, 51, 52, 53, 64, 68, 90, 101, 113, 134, 141
Austin American-Statesman: 72
Austin College: 17
Austin Country Club: 102
Austin High School (Reagan): 142

B

Bage, Carl: 22
Ball High School (Galveston): 132, 133
Baltimore Colts: 78, 97
Barrett, Clyde: 6
Barron, David: xv, 112
Barton Springs: xvi
Baton Rouge, Louisiana: 107, 130, 135
Battle of the Coral Sea: 15
Baylor University: 25, 129
Bealle, David: 79
Bean, Bubba: xii, 82, 97
Beaumont, Texas: 2
Beauty: 11
Bell High School, L. D. (Hurst): 79
Bellard, Debra: 51, 143
Bellard, Emory Jr.: xx, 22, 51, 141, 142, 143
Bellard, Louie Cass: 3, 142
Bellard, Mary Kay: 21, 22, 112, 141
Bellard, Norman: 3, 14, 15, 16
Bellard, Pearl: 3, 15
Bellard, Pug: 3, 15, 16
Bellard, Robert "Bob": 51, 111, 143
Bellard, Susan: v, xii, 26, 108, 141, 142
Berry Creek Country Club: 141
Bertelsen, Jim: xviii, 55
Bible, Dana X.: 19, 20, 22
Big Country Athletic Hall of Fame: 32, 145, 148
Big Spring, Texas: 20
Birmingham, Alabama: 108, 135
Birmingham News: 107
Bishop Junior High School: 25, 26
Blair, Sam: 82
Blaschke, O. T.: 24.
Blocker, Dan: 53
Blount, Peppy: 20
Bluebonnet Bowl: 96, 126, 147
Bobcat Athletic Hall of Fame, San Angelo, Texas: 145
Bobcat Stadium: 142
Bobcats (San Angelo High School): 47, 48, 50
Bond, John: 107, 135, 136

Boston Harbor: 15
Bradley, Bill: ix, 61, 62, 63, 68, 69
Brazil: 128
Brazosport, Texas: 16
Breazeale, George: 72
Breckenridge, Texas: 29, 30, 32, 33, 34, 35, 36, 40, 41, 45, 100
Breckenridge American: 32, 33, 36
Breckenridge High School: xiii, xvi, xvii, xviii, 26, 27, 29, 30, 31, 32, 33, 34, 35, 36, 37, 38, 41, 44, 45, 51, 54, 55, 71, 72, 81, 99, 100, 116, 117, 119, 122, 146, 148
Briles, Art: xiii
Brown, James: 45
Brown, Mack: 72
Browning, Azel: 14, 15
Brownwood High School: xiii, 38, 39
Bryan-College Station, Texas: 79, 82
Bryan High School: 143
Bryant, Paul "Bear": xi, 54, 64, 66, 77, 85, 105, 106, 107, 112
Buchanan Dam: 27
Buckaroos (Breckenridge High School): xii, 31, 33, 34, 35
Bujnoch, Glenn: 97
Bull, Ronnie: 25, 26
Bulldogs (Mississippi State University): 105, 106, 143
Bullington, Wally: 77
Burson, Rusty: 77, 80
Burton, Richard: 53
Buxkemper, Jerome "Bux": 20, 21

C
Caldwell County, Texas: 4
Camp Longhorn: 27, 129
Campbell, Dave: xiv
Dave Campbell's Texas Football magazine: xiv, xxi, 145, 148
Campbell, Earl: 126, 132
Campbell, Mike: xvii, xix
Canning, Whit: 63
Central High School (see San Angelo High School)
Cherry, Blair: 19, 22
Cincinnati Bengals: 97
Cincinnati University: x

Clarion Ledger/Jackson Daily News: 106
Cleburne High School: 34, 39, 40, 51
Cleveland, Rick: 106
Coastal Bend Coaches Association: 145
College Football Hall of Fame: 145
College Station, Texas: 77, 80, 103, 112, 126, 143
Collins, Terry: 55, 123
Comanche High School: 30
Cooper, Gary: 15
Cooper High School (Abilene): 46, 123
Corpus Christi, Texas: 10, 22, 26, 29, 109
Corpus Christi Naval Station: 21
Cotton Bowl: x, xi, xii, 54, 63, 74, 77, 80, 81, 101, 106, 124
Cougars (University of Houston): x
Couk, Pete: 2
Courtney, Joe: 103
Cox, Jack: 29, 30
Creagh, Bill: 32, 33, 36
Crousen, Joe: 36, 38, 39
Crow, John David: 66
Culwell, John: 41

D
Dacy, Wayne: 49, 50
Dallas, Texas: 62, 101, 145
Daugherty, Duffy: 63
Davidson, Mrs.: 90
Davis, Greg: 72
Davis Hill: 3, 4, 5, 6, 9, 12
Davis, Joe: 22
DeBerry, Fisher: 68
Delmar Junior College: 22, 23
Dickey, Curtis: 82, 95
Dilworth, Emory: 1
Doerr, Timmy: 39
Dove, Mark: 47
Dowdie, Mike: 37
Donald Duck: 5
Dulcita: 141

E
Edwards, Dooley: 23
El Paso, Texas: 92, 94, 95
Ellington, Bill: xvii

Emerson, Ox: 22, 23, 139
Erxleben, Russell: 129, 130

F

Fairbanks, Chuck: 67
Feller, Happy: 129
Fields, Edgar: xii, 82, 97
Florida, University of: 92, 93, 95, 96, 129
Florida State University: x
Fox, Wayne: 123
Franklin, Tony: xii, 82, 93, 129, 130
Freedom Bowl: 108

G

Galveston, Texas: 2, 132
Galveston Ball High School (see Ball High
    School)
Gandy, Travis: 39
Garrison, Punk: 24

George, Leonard: 110, 111
Georgetown, Texas: xii, 108, 141, 144, 148
Georgia, University of: 136
Gibbs, Sonny: 37
Gibson, Jerry: 36, 38, 40
Gilbert, Chris: xviii, 63
Golding, Joe: 44
Gonzales, Texas: 1, 7
Flash Gordon: 6
Goswick, Bobby: 32
Graham High School: 30, 37
Gray, Tim: 82
Greater Houston Football Coaches
    Association: 145
Gulf of Mexico: 10, 11

H

Hagan, Bo: ix
Hahn, Freddie: 24
Hamilton, Buddy: 37
Hansen, Jeffrey: 25, 26
Harbor Island, Texas: 10, 13, 14
Hardin-Simmons University: 148
Harmon, Mark: 64
Harmon, Tom: 64
Harrison, Bob: 32
Hatfield, Kenny: 68
Haugen, Robert: 24, 25

Hayes, Lester: xii, 82, 132, 133, 134, 135
Hebronville High School: 24
Heisman Trophy: 64, 66
Herndon, Mr.: 12
Herskowitz, Mickey: 53, 126
Houston, Texas: 46, 112, 113, 132, 139
Houston, University of: x, 61, 62, 63, 132
Houston, U.S.S.: 15
Houston Chronicle: xv, 23, 47, 112, 126
Houston Oilers: 97
Houston Post: 53
Houston Touchdown Club: 145
Houston Wheatley High School
    (see Wheatley High School)
Huddleston, Charles: 36
Humble, Texas: 26, 79, 109
Humble High School: 79, 110, 111
Huntsville High School: 110
Hurst L. D. Bell High School (see L. D. Bell
    High School)

I

Ingleside High School: 26, 27, 29, 30, 33, 41
Inks Lake: 27
Island Cottages: 9

J

Jackson, Charlie: 14
Jackson, Mrs.: 14
Jackson, Mississippi: xi, 105
Jackson, Robert: 79
Japan: 21
Java:, 15, 16
Jay, Mike: 79, 80
Jennings, Waylon: 53
Johnson, Red: 47
Jones, Grady: 24
Jones Stadium: xi

K

Kansas, University of: 108
Kansas City Chiefs: 97
Katy High School: 111
Kennedy, Robert "Bobby": xvi
Kerbel, Joe: 31, 33
Kimberlin, Larry: 36, 39
King, Joe: 12, 13
King, J. T.: ix

King, Martin Luther Jr.: xvi
Kingsville, Texas: 2, 33, 36
Kingsville High School (H. M. King): 2, 22, 32, 33, 34, 35
Kingsville Record: 36
Kingwood, Texas: 109, 111
Koy, Ted: xviii
Kugiya, Hugo: 54
Kyle Field: 82, 85, 86, 87

L
L. D. Bell High School (Hurst): 79
Lake Austin: 100
Lane, Jorvorskie: 122
Laney, Lindy: 12
Las Vegas, Nevada: 77
Layne, Bobby: 128
Layne, Rob: 128
Leaks, Roosevelt: 63
Lee High School (Midland): 49
Liberty Bowl: xii, 80, 81
Lighthouse Cottages: 11
Little, Steve: 129, 130
Little Rock, Arkansas: xii
Little Southwest Conference: 45, 77
Lone Ranger: 6
Longhorns (University of Texas): ix, x, xi, xvi, 63, 67, 112, 143
Los Angeles Coliseum: 125
Louisiana: 25, 79
LSU (Louisiana State University): xi, 104, 106, 107, 130, 136
Love, Mike: 49
Lubbock, Texas: ix
Luling, Texas: xiii, 1, 3, 4, 5, 6, 7, 14

M
Maddox, Carl: 104
Marble Falls, Texas: 112, 113
Marblehead, U.S.S.: 15
Massey, Billy Fred: 26, 122
Massey, John: 26, 122
McCallum, Napoleon: 104
McClellan, Mike: 32
McCrumbly, Joe Bob: 79
McKay, John: 81
McKinney High School: 32

McMurray, Bill: 47
McNamara, Tom: 12
McWilliams, David: 39
Mehaffey, Maurice: 122
Memorial Stadium (now Darrell K. Royal Memorial Stadium): xvi, 47, 68, 69, 105
Michigan, University of: 27
Michigan State University: x, 63, 64
Midland Lee High School (see Lee High School)
Moore, Dana: 130
Moser, Chuck: 77, 148
Mosley, Mike: 79, 96
Mickey Mouse: 5
Middlebrooks, Jack: 49
Milburn, Bob: 46
Mildren, Jack: 46
Mississippi State University: x, xi, xii, xiii, xv, 38, 94, 104, 105, 106, 107, 108, 109, 130, 135, 136, 143, 148
Moore, Carlos: 12
Mullins, Gary: 47, 123
Mustang Bowl: 32
Mustang Island, Texas: 10, 11, 13, 16
Myers, Jim: 44, 77

N
National Football Foundation: 145
Naval Academy, U.S. (Navy): 68, 104
Navy, U.S.: 7, 15, 16, 104
Navasota, Texas: xvii, 109
Nebraska, University of: 108
Nederland High School: 32
Nelson, Willie: 53
Nixon, Richard: x

O
Oakland Raiders: 134, 135
Odessa High School: 31
Odessa Permian High School (see Permian High School)
Ogilvie, Major: 107
Oklahoma, University of: 49, 62
Oklahoma State University: 53, 54, 62
Orange Blossom Special: 47, 48
Osborne, Richard: xii, 82, 97
Owens, Steve: 128

P

Padre Island, Texas: 10, 11, 29
Palestine High School: 61
Pampa High School: 79
Parker, Fess: 53
Parker, Larry: 36
Parrington, Tim: 135, 136
Pearl Harbor: 15
Permian High School (Odessa): 46, 49, 79, 142
Pesch, Joe Ed: 36
Peterson, Pete: 43
Philadelphia Eagles: 61, 97
Phillips, Eddie: 55, 63, 68, 69, 112
Pitzer, Bill: 36
Pitzer, P.W. "Trey" III: 36
Port Aransas, Texas: 2, 7, 9, 10, 11, 12, 16, 17
Port Isabel, Texas: 10
Powell, Dee: 74, 132, 133
Pro Bowl: 97, 134
Pro Football Hall of Fame: 134

Q

R

Rapoport, Ian R.: 107
Razorbacks (University of Arkansas): xii, 80
Red Raider Sports Magazine: 148
Red Raiders (Texas Tech University): ix, x
Reynolds Company: 2+
Rice University: ix, 22, 96
Rio Grande Valley: 22
Roaches, Carl: xii, 82, 97
Robbins, Cooper: 31, 33
Roberts, W. H.: 36
Robertson, Tex: 27, 28
Robstown High School: 22
Rodgers, Dickie: 36, 39, 122
Rogers, Pepper: 64
Roosevelt, Franklin Delano: 10, 15
Rose Bowl: 80
Royal, Darrell K.: ix, x, xvi, xvii, xix, xx, 50, 51, 52, 54, 61, 62, 63, 64, 65, 67, 69, 71, 72, 74, 81, 89, 106, 112, 127, 128, 131, 143

S

Saban, Nick: xii, 108
St. Mary's University: 13

Samson, Chuck: 78
San Angelo, Texas: 43, 47, 48, 50
San Angelo High School: xii, xvi, 27, 28, 44, 45, 46, 47, 48, 49, 50, 51, 52, 67, 71, 72, 81, 99, 119, 122, 123, 141, 142, 143, 146, 148
San Angelo Standard Times: 46, 51, 77, 145
San Antonio, Texas: 13, 14, 139, 145
San Marcos, Texas: 21
Schwarz, Blake: 97
Scribner, Mr.: 13, 16
Seattle Times: 54
Sherman, Texas: 17
Shipman, David: 79
Shotwell, Pete: 33
Simmler, Melvin: 6
Simonini, Ed: xii, 77, 78, 82, 97
Sizemore, Jerry: 138
Slocum, R. C.: 81, 112
Snead, Sam: 16
Sooners (University of Oklahoma): 67
South America: 128
South Pacific: 15
Southeastern Conference: 106
Southern California, University of: 65, 80, 81, 96, 106, 126
Southwest Conference: ix, x, xi, 22, 63, 72, 76, 78, 79, 80, 81, 91, 101, 106, 129, 132, 139, 148
Southwest Texas State University: 21, 139, 145
Spears, Bob "Little Bob": 99, 100, 101, 102
Spectrum Scoreboards: 115, 117, 118
Speyrer, Cotton: 124, 138
Sporting News: 145
Spring Branch School District: 68, 139
Spring High School: 47, 68
Spring Westfield High School (see Westfield High School)
Stallings, Gene: 71, 77, 81
Starkville, Mississippi: xi, xii, 104, 107, 108, 143
Stephens, Jack: 40
Stephenville High School: xiii
Story of Dr. Wassell, The: 15
Street, James: x, 61, 62, 63, 68, 69

Sun Bowl: 92, 94, 95, 108, 129, 147
Super Bowl: 134
Sweetwater, Texas: 32
Sweetwater High School: 32, 36
Switzer, Barry: 67

T

Tabor, Mike: 122
Tascosa High School (Amarillo): 47, 51
Tarpon Inn: 10
Taylor, Bill: 122
Taylor, Elizabeth: 53
Ten Naple, Garth: 79, 97, 112
Tennessee, University of: 63, 104, 124
Texas, University of: xi, xv, xv, xvi, 19, 20, 27,
    39, 51, 52, 53, 55, 62, 68, 71, 72, 74, 89,
    90, 100, 101, 112, 119, 127, 141, 143, 148
Texas A&M Athletic Hall of Fame: 84, 145
Texas A&M University: xi, xii, xiii, xv, xvi, x,
    xvii, 20, 43, 44, 66, 71, 72, 74, 75, 76, 77,
    78, 79, 80, 81, 82, 83, 84, 85, 86, 87, 88,
    89, 90, 91, 92, 93, 95, 96, 97, 102, 103,
    104, 106, 107, 109, 112, 122, 126, 129,
    132, 133, 134, 143, 145, 147, 148
Texas High School All-Star Game: 145
Texas High School Coaches Association: 15,
    75, 81, 145
Texas Sports Hall of Fame: 62, 115, 118, 145
Texas Tech University: ix, x, 61, 62
Thomas, Pat: xii, 76, 82, 97
Tidehaven High School: 24
Tome, Kim: 95
Trussell, Jake: 33, 36
Tulane University: x
Tuscaloosa, Alabama: 64, 65, 105
12th Man Magazine: 77, 80, 97

U

UCLA (University of California, Los
    Angeles): 47
University of Texas Sports News Service: 52

V

Valdosta, Georgia: 135
Victoria High School: 22
Villa Capri: 53

W

Waco, Texas: 12, 33, 115, 145, 148
Wadzeck, G. B.: 50
Wake Forest: : x
Walker, Alvin "Skip": 97
Walker, Bobby: 36
Walker, David: 79
Walkover, The: 84
Washington, D.C.: 10, 134
Webb, Ernest: 7
Welch, Bruce: 97
Westfield High School (Spring): xiii, xv, 109,
    110, 111, 112, 117, 143, 147, 148
Westmoreland College: 14
West Point, U.S. Military Academy at
    (Army): 68, 103, 104
Wheatley High School (Houston): 132, 133,
    134
Wichita Falls High School: 32, 40, 44, 122
Wigginton, Donnie: 47, 63, 68, 69, 74, 112
Wilkinson, Bud: 54
Williams, Jack: 75, 96
Williams, Jackie: 97
Wilson, Jimmo: 36
Wilson's Marina: 10
Wood, Gordon: xiii, 32
Wood, Russ: 107
Woodard, George: xii, 82, 96, 126
Woodmen's Hall: 11
Woods, Tiger: 140
Woodsboro High School: 51, 24, 106
Worster, Steve: ix, x, xviii, 55, 67, 125
Wright, Bobby Ray: 24
Wright, Jimmy: 40

Y

Yarborough, Ralph W.: 48
Yeager, Mr.: 14
Yeoman, Bill: x
Young, John Paul: 74, 77

Z

Zimmatore, Billy: 23